We Gave Then.

Life,

Now They're Trying To Take

Ours

How To Talk To Adult Children
Before It's Too Late

ERIC ROBESPIERRE

Copyright © 2019 by Eric Robespierre.

All rights reserved. No part of this publication may be reproduced, distributed, or transmitted in any form or by any means, including photocopying, recording, or other electronic or mechanical methods, without the prior written permission of the publisher, except in the case of brief quotations embodied in critical reviews and certain other noncommercial uses permitted by copyright law.

Library of Congress Control Number: 2019910440
ISBN: 978-0-578-53955-3

Published by Eric Robespierre
www.ericrobespierre.com

Also by Eric Robespierre

The Yummy Hunter's Guide
The Best-Tasting, Low-Calorie Foods
and Where to Shop for Them
(With Helen Brand)

Cracking the Walnut
How Being a Little Nuts Helped Me
to Beat Prostate Cancer

Living Large in America
The Life and Times of the Family
Ginsburg (pronounced Du Pont)

Lighten Up and Log In For Love
How Humor Helps Baby Boomers Survive Online Dating

Acknowledgments

We Gave Them Life, Now They're Trying to Take Ours, could not have been written without the support and wisdom of the parents who so graciously, honestly and sometime painfully opened up their hearts and souls to me. They did it so other parents could benefit from their experiences. I wish to thank my copyeditor and proofreader, Jennifer Henderson, and Marvin Lui who designed my cover and formatted this book for their outstanding professionalism and creativity.

This book is dedicated to all my distraught friends whose anguish inspired me to write this book and prove to them it's not their damn fault.

*The role of the parent is not to become the child,
but to provide guidance to walk it through the same abyss
the parents walked through but with the help of a light
called parental guidance.*

—Lamine Pearlheart

Contents

Acknowledgments v
Introduction xv

One
Still In The House (You Do What You Need to Do.) 1

Two
Their Marital Status (Landmine!) 9

Three
Your Marital Status (Part 1. The Divorce.) 24

Four
Your Marital Status (Part 2. A Mixed Bag.) 32

Five
Their Social Life (Mind Your Own Beeswax.) 38

Six
Your Social Life (You Have One…?) 47

Seven
Their Appearance (Looks Can Kill.) 52

Eight
Sibling Rivalry (One Is Not The Loneliest Number.) 59

Nine
Non-Biological (Same As It Ever Is.) 71

Ten
The Grandchildren (Want to see their Facebook Page?)...80

Eleven
Distance Makes The Heart Grow Sadder (Or Does It?)...93

Twelve
Downsizing (The Up Side.)..101

Thirteen
Your Finances (Wills Of The Wisp.) 107

Fourteen
Their Finances (Better Call Saul.)...................................112

Fifteen
Your Health (I Could Be Younger.)..................................121

Sixteen
Their Health (They Should Live And Be Well.) 127

Seventeen
Holidays (You In The Spirit?) 138

Eighteen
Vacations (Part 1. Togetherness.) 146

Nineteen
Vacations (Part 2. Home Alone?) 152

Twenty
Vacations (Part 3. Three Day Old Fish, etc…)................156

Twenty-One
In-laws (Don't Go There!) 160

Twenty-Two
Social Media (Kumbaya!)..167

Twenty-Three
Politics (The Elephant In The Room.) 174

Twenty-Four
Fact or Fiction (The Rashomon Effect.) 180

Twenty-Five
Cats Among The Pigeons (Mothers and Daughters) 194

Twenty-Six
She Walks On Water (Daddy's Little Girl) 198

Twenty-Seven
Death Comes To Us All (Hush, Hush.) 203

Twenty-Eight
The Takeaway (Before They Take Us Away, Away.) 208

About the Author 226

Introduction
(Skip at Your Own Peril.)

You're only as happy as your saddest child.

—Anonymous, mother of one

I owe the writing of this book to a perfectly innocent encounter with a friend whose sudden venting gave way to a burst of pent up angst that set me back on my heels.

Her story enfolded thusly. That morning, she had called her daughter, as she frequently does, and just to make conversation inquired as to her weekend plans. The daughter confessed her boyfriend had canceled and she would be alone for the next two days. My friend, innocently and without malice or a hidden agenda, responded by saying, "Oh, that's too bad."

With that, the daughter unexpectedly and angrily lashed out. "What? You don't think I can be alone? That's why I hate you! You never think I can handle things!"

Click! The daughter hung up and so began the lamentations, the recriminations and the guilt, the accumulation of which reached its boiling point when she met me.

My friend gathered her emotions, and with all seriousness said, she should have taken my advice and just… ZIPPED IT! Before I could console her she said, "You're a writer, why don't you write a book telling all parents that the best way to handle their kids is to just zip it?"

I didn't think much about her suggestion as I was busy with publishing my latest book, but the idea resonated with me. I knew from personal experience too many of my friends, myself included, could use a little help in better communicating with their adult children. Naturally, to just 'zip it', while it might work in certain situations, was just a single course of action. Surely, there were others and perhaps I could gather them up for an advice book? To proceed, I decided to interview as many parents of adult children as I could to learn how they communicate with their kids. What were their secrets to having an open and honest, and loving, two-way relationship with their kids and by association, spouses, grandchildren and extended family members?

In the last two years, I have heard tales of happiness, hardship and heartache. The interviews expanded my perspective and provided unique insight into the true nature of how tricky, and emotionally perilous, communicating with adult children can be for parents, even in our golden years when we are supposed to be so wise.

Laugh, and the world laughs with you;
Weep, and you weep alone.

—Ella Wheeler Wilcox

If my interviews were to be successful, I had to put my subjects at ease. I told them I was looking for answers that might help ME because I had two adult kids and I didn't want to screw up my relationship with them. I injected a little humor directed at the absurdity of the relationships we have with our kids, hoping it would further relax my interviewees so their 'true confessions' would end with laughter and not tears. I tried to do the same in my book. To help me get my point across, I sought the wit and wisdom from Confucius to George Carlin, whose quotes sum up each chapter.

I want to thank the dozen or so mothers and fathers who so candidly opened their hearts and souls to me. I understand it's a small, and by no means, definitive analysis of the problems we all face, but their experiences are most enlightening. One thing is certain—none of us are alone in our suffering. The trials and tribulations we endure are shared by anyone who is a parent of an adult child.

I hope by taking these experiences to heart, it will enable you, the reader, to sustain, improve or even mend your relationship with your adult children.

One final thought. When we're met with frustrations so intolerable and we check our children's birth certificates to make sure these Alien Beings came from our loins, just remember the first time they looked up at us from their cribs and smiled. (No, damn it—it wasn't gas!)

Regardless of your good intentions, whatever you do, be prepared that it will be wrong.

Anonymous, mother of two

It's not a perfect world and you can't be expected to provide a perfect family.

Anonymous, mother of two

Eric Robespierre

*What I am most interested in is what makes
our kids tick. I can't figure it out.*

> Anonymous, father of six

*When my kids were born I made the strict determination
I would not take the credit or the blame for their lives.*

> M, mother of four

*So much craziness with my daughter,
it sent me back to therapy.*

> Anonymous, mother of two

*Two successful children and I have a good
relationship with both. I give nature the kudos.*

> S, mother of two

*My handling wasn't quite good enough and I have to
face the consequences, but I also tell them I did the
best I could, considering my traditions, my hang-ups.*

> Anonymous, mother of two

I gave them all the tools and as much support as we could, then, and now. A college education without having to pay back any student loans, babysitting when they needed it, and we listen to their problems. We are secure in knowing they know how to take care of themselves and they know we very much have a life of our own.

J, mother of six

I tell him—he responds, good, bad, or indifferent. My therapist says it's very easy to get along with a clone.

Anonymous, mother of two

You should never criticize. Never say boo. If your child strangles someone you should say, good job honey! (Laughs)

B, mother of one

I was hovering too much and he was resentful, took it out by being angry with me. I know it was because he was a twin and I lost the other one. Not an excuse, but we are all human.

P, mother of two

Eric Robespierre

Do the best you can as a parent and whatever happens, happens.

M, mother of four

I see my mom as a great mom and I see everything I didn't do as a mom. I don't know, maybe I'm too hard on myself.

B, mother of one

I'd move if I could afford it and if they weren't so good at tracking me down.

GY, mother of two

I take no credit and all the blame. Of course, I need a shrink, but at my age (69 and counting backwards), can't see how that would help.

BC, mother of two

My daughter moved in with her boyfriend. He gives her rings, says he's going to marry her. I don't question her as long as they're happy. They have their bumps—everyone has bumps. I just listen.

N, mother of two

They develop in a certain way and what is, is.

M, mother of four

I turned his room into an Airbnb and you'd have thought I disowned him.

CL, mother of one

My mother was very controlling and I made up my mind, whatever my kids did with their own lives was OK.

Anonymous, mother of four

The eldest, she's a bit of a nutcase. The middle one is the nicest. She calls me all the time. The youngest lives the closest, but ignores me. She ran away once. They're all there for me though. I'm really lucky to have them.

Anonymous, mother of three

I love all my children, but I don't like them all.

J, mother of six

I only used whole words.

GG, father of three

Boys are so different. Have a disagreement, no repercussions. If it's over, it's over.

B, mother of two

I saw too many families where mothers took credit or blame. That was not a healthy thing to do. Much healthier to let them alone and be their own people.

M, mother of four

When she was ready to exhibit control, we let her. It's carried through in her life, certainly.

W, mother of two

I wanted to give them two gifts: independence and to like themselves.

J, mother of six

I talk to my daughter about her beliefs that I think are irrational, but it's no use. She's been brainwashed. Now, she has kids and is brainwashing them. I'm even more upset, figuring out how to deal with that development.

Anonymous, father of three

She knows I want to have a relationship with her but she's angry with me. So, I'm not pressing her. I'm standing back.

B, mother of two

They had to be independent. It was a matter of having lots of kids, no real finances. They were going to the dentist by themselves when they were six years old. It was a different city then. They could go anywhere by themselves.

Anonymous, mother of four

With many of my contemporaries, the problems with their kids are deeply psychological or psychiatric. They need to be handled by professionals. Even then, it may not do any good. Some of my friends have given up. That's my observation. Could I let go? Probably not...

C, mother of four

My job is to love them and then get them out.

P, mother of three

You cannot control your children when they become adults. Then, when they're in their forties or fifties, forget about it. (Laughter)

Anonymous, mother of three

I think a good relationship with your children is based on your expectations. My girls are very different. They were like that from childhood so I always had different expectations for each and as a result, I have never been disappointed.

M, mother of two

Working with five-year-olds taught me a lot about adults, because at five, all their characteristics are exposed, but as they grow into adults they become hidden. I try to remember this, remember those five-year-old characteristics when I look into the faces of my forty-year-olds.

Anonymous, mother of two

You can say what they are, what they have become has been somewhat determined by what we gave them in our home, in their childhood. If so, we are still responsible.

Anonymous, mother of two

As parents we brought them into this world, they did not have a choice. But, as they grow into adults, we have to respect the fact that now they have choices.

Anonymous, mother of two

There isn't a limit on age, where we can say that's it and you're on your own. A parent's commitment, responsibility to that child, and its needs, never ends.

Anonymous, mother of two

I don't believe in giving them a pass, and I didn't because it would have provided them with a way out later on in life.

Anonymous, father of three

I believe advice between most people, and this is even truer in a parent and child relationship, falls on deaf ears. I don't mean you stop talking to your children, however, if there is a serious problem, it's good to have a third person, someone objective, because kids don't hear a parent as loud as they would someone that doesn't have that personal history with them. Of course, if you can manage it, someone professional might be the solution.

Anonymous, mother of two

I always thought that once she had a child of her own, she would appreciate me more. Unfortunately, she can't have a child and doesn't want to adopt. Guess I have to have new expectations, huh?

Anonymous, mother of one

Eric Robespierre

It's human nature to take care of the things you love.

C, mother of three

Both my children left the house right after college, as did my husband and I in our families. I'm not sure if their behavior came from their identifying with our history, or from their own needs? Or is it a combination?

Anonymous, mother of two

I'm your mother, not your friend. And I stuck to it. You have to have boundaries.

Anonymous, mother of two

Kids follow their friends, see stuff on TV, have free minds, free will and will do what they do and you can't always assume you are to blame for that. To improve relationships, you cannot blame yourself, because if you do, you will try to fix it and it's not your job.

Anonymous, mother of two

Their character, personality comes from us and of course nature, but the nurture part is what we can control. If we could have done better, through no fault of our own, we must see what we can offer now. There is still room for growth, for all of us.

Anonymous, mother of two

You're fortunate to get what you get.

Anonymous, mother of two

Stick to your principles, follow what you think is the right thing to do and love them truly.

N, mother of two

> *If your kid needs a role model and you ain't it, you're both fucked.*
>
> —George Carlin, *Brain Droppings*

One

Still In The House
(You Do What You Need to Do.)

He's the flesh of my flesh.

—Anonymous, mother of three

"You can't go home again." I think if Thomas Wolfe were alive today he might amend that famous line as a confluence of current events seem to conspire to force a significant number of adult children to do the exact opposite and return home.

One parent told me she was just thankful it was only because he lost his job and not because of any substance abuse problem.

Another welcomed her fifty-year-old home after his most recent divorce, confessing this was his pattern, understanding there was nothing she or her husband could do, except provide him with comfort and support, until he went back across country and presumably resumed his errant ways.

Another parent recounted that since his son graduated college twenty years ago, he travels to a distant country, pays his expenses by tutoring the local kids in English, and after five or so years, returns to his old room and hangs out for a few months, then heads out again. Several times he and his wife wanted to downsize and move to an apartment in the city, but guilt made them deny themselves this opportunity.

May I suggest some rules? If you want them to leave, stop doing their laundry, ask for rent, and if all else fails, list their room on Airbnb. If you want them to stay, don't lock the door at midnight and put them on a meal plan.

On a daily basis, he'd only cook for himself. Irony is he's a great sous chef. When I asked him why he didn't cook for us he said he didn't feel an obligation to cook for anyone else.

Anonymous, mother of three

Him coming home wasn't easy. It was the best thing for him. The best thing for me because I was always worried about him, being so far away, having to put his son into daycare. Being without his family.

Anonymous, mother of three

I have been accused of taking a backseat when I didn't object to him coming back after his divorce. True, but it was the safest place in the house.

Anonymous, father of four

My mother took me in after an ugly divorce. I'd do the same if it came to that with any of my kids.

KJ, father of three

No matter how tight our housing situation, it would never be too tight for any of my kids. I think they know that and that's why one of them said, "Mom, I will never put you in a home."

H, mother of three

Leave notes for us. Be respectful. One day we see a note. Going out, won't be back till eleven. Going to get laid.

C, mother of two

I was happy to have her and our two grandkids stay with me for as long as it takes. We're also lucky we have the room and finances. If we had to go in debt, we would have made it work.

S&L, parents of four

Where is my son going to go? I don't know? I gave him plenty of warning, telling him I'm selling the house. I'm going to miss my grandkids.

L, mother of three

At the moment my daughter can't make ends meet, but she's close to getting herself straightened out, so I'm just glad I can help. It's what parents do.

LL, single mother of two

Don't question their motives, give advice, or ask for how long until the dust settles. If they want you to listen, you listen. If they want advice, give it with the caveat it's their life and they must do what they believe is right for them. Finally, have an honest discussion of how this new arrangement is impacting your life and what the future holds for all of you.

B, mother of one

You have to live under your parents' rule as long as you live under their roof. So, I had no problem with my son when he came home after his divorce.

Anonymous, mother of three

This doesn't exactly apply, but both girls came back after college and stayed with me until one got married and the other moved in with her future husband. Two to three years, I think. They were very responsible. I do miss sitting with them on the couch.

M, mother of two

Guess I'm old-fashioned. You only moved out of the house when you got married and you never moved back. Now, all sorts of problems bring them home, and you must take them in, and take care of them, until they get back on their feet.

N, mother of four

It took him six months to a year until I finally convinced him to move back with my one-year-old grandson. He lived with us for three years until he re-married. He now has another son, and he and his entire family live just a few miles away.

M, mother of three

I had no choice. He had a bad divorce, no place else to go, so I ended up having an adult son living in my house that didn't like the ground rules. Basically, I disapproved of every single thing he did. We both lived through it.

Anonymous, mother of three

Eric Robespierre

He lived at home with us after a half year of college. When his drinking issues surfaced I had no problem, but my husband did because his mother told him once you're living on your own, it won't be good for you to lose that independence. I thought that was too hard and fast a rule, maybe worked for my husband, but not for my son. My husband finally came around and accepted the situation.

Anonymous, mother of three

They both stayed in the house with us for six months after their college graduations to get themselves organized and then they left, got jobs, their own apartments.

Anonymous, mother of two

There are times when you think you're not judging them, but they think you are doing just that. They read it so wrong, so badly. Makes the situation hard when they come back.

Anonymous, mother of two

He was thirty-one when he moved out, finished his master's degree. He was a good kid, never a problem. Worked hard at school, was very aware of his place as an adult, not a child who had to be looked after. So, my husband and I stayed out of his life. We thought the older a child gets, if the parent tries to interfere by providing too much support, it can cripple the child and parents should stand back.

Anonymous, mother of two

I have a twenty-four-year-old daughter who lives in the house. She has a boyfriend about the same age who is always here as well. She wants to be an adult, but expects me to put the dinner on the table for them after I come home from work. I had to sit her down, draw the line, and tell her what I expect. Things have changed for the better.

Anonymous, mother of two

When he turned eighteen, I told him he was on his own. He went to college and never came back to live with me. I gave him money when I had it, didn't when I didn't. He had to man up. Had he been a girl, maybe I would have acted differently. You have to remember, I had raised him without a father.

Anonymous, mother of one

I probably have the strangest story. I was separated and divorced for fifteen years and during that time my daughters, who were in their thirties, moved in and out until I got back together with my ex and remarried him about ten years later. They were very respectful and adult in taking their responsibilities seriously. We became closer, a real unit. Considering how rebellious they were when they were teenagers, all I can say is how blessed I am.

Anonymous, mother of two

He didn't give us any problem, but he was never part of the family. More like a ghost, a phantom. Despite that, we liked it because with him living in the house with us, we had a family unit and we were whole. He just left, age thirty-five, and now he reaches out to us. I have no answers for it.

Anonymous, mother of three

> *Have a little faith in your sons.
> This journey will be the making of them.*
>
> —C.J. Milbrandt,
> *On Your Marks: The Adventure Begins*

Two

Their Marital Status
(Landmine!)

They are living in sin!
Of course, I kept my mouth shut.
—C, father of three

My behavior has always been influenced, probably in an unrealistic way, by movies. After watching *Miracle on Thirty Four Street,* I knew HE was watching and HE'D know if I was naughty or nice. *Strangers on a Train* taught me never to have eye contact with anyone on a subway. And *Predator*, ah *Predator*—what did it teach me? Like the man said so wisely, "There's something out there waiting for us, and it ain't no man. We're all gonna die." Obviously, he was talking about asking your kids about their marriage!

One mother told me that after her daughter complained that her husband was suddenly coming home from work later than usual, she went so far as to purchase a tracking device to put on her son-in-law's car. When she later learned his schedule had changed because he'd given up driving in favor of taking a train, she joked she was happy her suspicions didn't lead her into hiring a hit man.

Another mother told me her daughter-in-law hates her and had formed a wedge between her and her son, causing them not to speak. This was because she erroneously believed when the boy was an infant, she never picked him up from the crib and let him cry for hours. A stream of vulgarities followed and threats of kidnapping made me move on to another subject. (More on in-laws and memories of bad parenting in later chapters.)

One father of two married girls said he gave them both a wide berth while they were growing up, trusting them to do the right and proper thing. Both turned out fine with long and happy marriages. He did confess he prayed a lot and, on several occasions, resisted the impulse to throw assorted unsavory-looking suitors out a window.

By now, you can see where this book is headed. There will be no easy answers, certainly, none that fits all. But hope springs eternal and perhaps one parent's story will resonate and help you resolve whatever conflicts you face.

Remember, you taught them to be independent thinkers, not terrorists, so forget the axiom: *If you see something, say something.*

*I have a child who will never marry.
I know I have to accept that...*

P, mother of two

You ever heard of 'intentional infliction of emotional distress?' It's grounds for divorce. Well, that's what's going on with me, and my daughter-in-law, only I can't divorce her if you know what I mean.

Anonymous, mother of one

He must be great in bed because he's certainly not up to her intellectual standards. Other things in common make up for it, I guess. I bite the bullet, keep it all inside. I don't want to run the risk of losing my daughter. Who wouldn't do what I do if they were in my position?

Anonymous, mother of three

He's nice to the kids, nice to me. So what if I wouldn't have picked him for her? Who knows if it's permanent? I bet it won't be.

Anonymous, mother of two

No matter whom he brought home, I loved her because I wanted him to be happy.

P, mother of two

Eric Robespierre

She came to my sixtieth birthday with a handsome guy, but she never went beyond an informal introduction. I had no idea she was thinking of marrying him.

Anonymous, mother of one

They were separated for three years and now they're back together. I drop the subject of why, like a hot potato. I think it's because of the kids. Wants to be a part of their lives and a divorce would have prevented it, or at least taken away a lot of his day-to-day overseeing of their lives.

Anonymous, mother of two

I try to look at their problems objectively, see both sides, and then I give my opinion. That's as far as I can go. I always end by saying this is your life. You have to make the final decision. I'm going to my house. I don't have the problems sitting on me.

J, mother of six

We don't talk about her problems, but at least she knows that she has a mother who came out the other end of a divorce okay.

Anonymous, mother of one

I think the reason he was divorcing my daughter was he had a girlfriend. I don't know that for a fact. I say nothing.

Anonymous, mother of one

I didn't know anything about their divorces. They didn't tell me until after it was over. I was never divorced, so I had no advice, anyway.

Anonymous, mother of eight

She said, "Mom, I do not want you to solve my problems. Just leave me alone." Can a mother change her daughter's personality? I don't think so.

B, mother of one

It was never our intention to say anything, but it was obvious from the start that we were going to have trouble with our son-in-law, or should I say I was. It was only because his family environment was so harsh and he never knew what a healthy, loving, hugging and kissing family was until we, I—wore him down. In the beginning, he was afraid to go into the refrigerator without first asking permission. Now it's a race to see who gets up earlier to get first dibs on the leftovers.

M, mother of two

She has shut everyone out. I say nothing because I respect her. Do I think she is doing the wrong thing? Absolutely. Hiding in the basement, feeling sorry for yourself isn't going to do jack shit. Another thing, she never asked for legal help. Me, who has gone through two divorces and came out better than okay on the other end. And she knows that!

Anonymous, mother of one

I was sure my second husband's adult daughter was gay, but he never believed me. I was smart enough never to say anything to her. I would never say anything negative to any of his kids. Are you crazy? They're his kids. You never do that.

S, mother of one, stepmother of three

I got three kids. My daughter's unmarried, with one kid. I don't know who the father is. I never asked because I knew she wouldn't say. You learn not to push. One son has three wives. I'm not sure if he's married any but he has three kids. He's also closemouthed. Like I said, you learn to just go along. My other son is married, no grandkids.

Anonymous, mother of three

Oh, I know my son is married. We had a close relationship before... now... well... it's getting better. You won't believe this, but about two months ago I got a terrible sick feeling. I knew something was wrong with my son. I was afraid to call because I knew he'd think I was a nut and the wife... well... it would give her another reason to keep me away. I finally went over, told him I had this feeling, and when he found out when it was, he said that was the same time he was thinking he needed to see me because he missed me. We keep our meetings secret and are talking more, from time to time.

Anonymous, mother of two

I was always cautious. I never wanted to say anything that his wife might not like.

Anonymous, stepmother of one

They came to us and we felt wanted. They wanted our support. One of our daughters called us every single day and twice on Sunday.

Anonymous, father of six

I wasn't happy with who they married, but nothing really serious in my objections. I said nothing, of course, and still don't.

Anonymous, mother of four

Eric Robespierre

Again, you have to know your kids and adjust your expectations. One called me as soon as she knew she was pregnant, the other waited six months. I understand that is the way it is.

M, mother of two

My mother was completely controlling and said—did, whatever she wanted and whatever came into her head. I reacted in the opposite way, no matter how upset I was when my daughter told me whom she wanted to marry.

Anonymous, mother of four

My son complained, confided he should have never gotten married, but I never agreed. I just tried to support him by saying he was very young when he made that decision. Of course, I knew it when it happened, but stuff like… 'I told you so', isn't going to help him get back on his feet. That kind of negativity is just harmful!

Anonymous, mother of three

Would I love to see my son in a loving relationship? Of course, but he'd rather stay in the marriage than risk a messy divorce, perhaps not seeing the kids on a regular basis, or because she may move out of state, marry somebody who might make it worse for my son. Who knows? Alright, I'm only thinking the worst, but he's such a good boy, I hate to see him not be able to have all the happiness in the world. What mother wouldn't?

Anonymous, mother of one

My son has the same sense of the ridiculous and we can say whatever we want to each other. No topic is off-limits. That includes his social life. I never say anything negative. (Laughs)

J, mother of two

My girls grew up hearing stories about my life and meeting their father and amazingly their lives parallel mine and that pleases me as well.

Anonymous, mother of two

He complains about his wife, silly thing. She's a bit of an airhead and both of us are more focused. I let him vent, then we laugh. Overall, she is exceptionally sweet and nice.

Anonymous, mother of two

I always had issues, didn't like his family, their values, work ethic. I didn't have problems with him in the beginning, but I figured the apple didn't fall far from the tree. I kept my mouth shut because I didn't think it was my place to interfere. Of course, now that they're getting a divorce I'm second-guessing myself.

Anonymous, mother of two

She never complained about the marriage, but I found it difficult to be around them. I said nothing. My fault because it ended up with me supporting them until, his lack of motivation among other issues, caused the divorce.

Anonymous, mother of two

You do things in your life because you obviously think it's the right way to. So, when your adult child comes home and announces she is having a child, but not marrying the father, it can cause one to have a rough time. She made her own decision. I had to make mine. My husband had a big problem with it, as well, but we knew we would not lose our daughter because of it. We both got over it.

Anonymous, mother of two

Being a teacher, it was hard to accept a son-in-law without an education. I knew I would never give up on my daughter, so I made sure not to object to their relationship.

Anonymous, mother of two

I know of a situation where the relationship has become irreparable to the point they broke off all contact because they were not happy with the person their daughter chose. I can see how miserable she and her husband are, but they refuse to budge. Thank God, she hasn't asked me for her opinion, because I made it a rule to never, ever judge another person's actions unless you have walked in their shoes, as the saying goes. I have put my arms around her and told her to be optimistic, that things will hopefully work out. I couldn't help myself.

Anonymous, mother of two

He's just been married a short while, but his wife has mother issues so, at this time, I don't have a good relationship with her, or with my son. I don't talk to him as much and when I do, it's strained. I will let it ride for now. Like my own mother told me, you have to play the cards you're dealt.

Anonymous, mother of three

When they were married, we did not dip our toe into that water. However, when they were going through their divorce, they came to us, and we gave them support, without judgment.

Anonymous, father of six

He wouldn't talk to me unless I read a book about mothers who did bizarre, criminal acts like locking their kids in cars and pushing them into a river and watching them drown. He didn't even read the book, the woman he lives with, and who doesn't even know me and who calls me Queen of the World, told him to read it.

Anonymous, mother of one

I'm not one to judge their choices. I was twenty-six, and thought I should be married and he was a lot of fun. And, he had a rent-controlled apartment. He turned out to be a sociopath.

Anonymous, mother of three

My son never married and has two children over their twenty-five-year relationship. I said my piece and that was it. I think if my husband had been alive they may have married because he could be very demanding, but I don't know. They were very persuasive; always saying they would do it, just give them time. No, it doesn't bother me because they have a very happy and loving life together and apparently you don't need a certificate for that.

Anonymous, mother of four

*When they talk to me about work, I give advice,
but when they talk to me about their husbands,
I am much more careful about saying anything.*

Anonymous, mother of two

*I had an open communications with him until the
women in his life took over and then not much.*

Anonymous, mother of three

*Try not to be judgmental, to be open, to be
available, to talk when things get tough.
To say, I'm here when you're ready.*

J, mother of two

*I don't need to know your sexual positions.
I'm your mother, not your friend.*

Anonymous, mother of three

I never bring it up because they are both happily married.

Anonymous, mother of two

I think what is important is to recognize they are not like us. My father and mother were happily married for sixty-one years. I had two husbands and my son, two wives. What do they say about second marriages? You marry someone like your first? Of course, you never see it. My son didn't either.

Anonymous, mother of one

I feel estranged, not part of his life. I always believed it was his wife, and maybe her family had something to do with it, but at fifty, he has a mind of his own, makes his own decisions so I can no longer blame them, or anyone else for his actions.

Anonymous, mother of two

How does the saying go? 'My son is my son until he gets him a wife. My daughter is my daughter for the rest of my life'. I should have had two daughters.

Anonymous, mother of two

They are adults. I may not always like their choices but my husband and I have tried, as best we could, not to interfere. It was tough with my daughter because at first we were not happy with her choice. But we got through it and it turned out that he's a terrific father and a loving and caring partner to my daughter.

Anonymous, mother of two

Never ever say, 'I told you so,' unless you want to spend the rest of your life trying to find out where they live.

The author, father of two

The natural state of the sentient adult is qualified unhappiness.

—F. Scott Fitzgerald, *The Crack Up*

Three

Your Marital Status
(Part 1. The Divorce.)

*We are all entitled to one mistake.
No, I've never told my kids that, or
how I feel about life, or their father.*

—J, mother of two

Writing this chapter was an eye-opener for me. It's not anything I learned from my adult children, but what I learned from other divorced parents. To a one, their response was unanimous: *They only think about what affects them!*

This was not said with any bitterness, regret, or as an accusation; only as a statement of what is, and what a divorced parent must accept if they hope to have a happy and loving relationship with their adult children.

Another topic of conversation was whether the divorce was amiable or filled with acrimony. If the parents kept their anger, hurt, recriminations or whatever misery to themselves: i.e., didn't badmouth the spouse ad infinitum… for the most part, peace reigned in providence and the parent/adult child relationships were positive.

If they chose to remember you were the one who tipped off the IRS to his offshore accounts, remind them you did visit him on his birthday.

Once my granddaughters were born, I invited my ex and his wife to Seders for the sake of the family. We don't have much to say to each other but, as I said, it's good for the grandkids.

Anonymous, mother of two

Take it from someone who's been there. It's one of the most damaging events in a child's life and even if they never show it, there is hurt and resentment and it's always about them.

K, mother of one

We sat them down, told them it was our decision and that it wasn't their fault. No problem. I see their father and his wife at family events. I know I'm lucky because most of my friends have had the opposite experience.

Anonymous, mother of two

My son-in-law went to live with his father. He blamed the mother. Thought the father walked on water, nothing was his fault. Still won't have anything to do with her and is a little distant when we interact even though my daughter keeps telling him I'm nothing like her.

Anonymous, mother of three

One Mother's Day I thanked his ex for sharing her son with me and letting him be a part of my life. She was surprised, but thanked me for being so good to him. I think our good relations was due in part to the fact never was a harsh word said in our family about her, or the divorce.

Anonymous, stepmother of one

When I split from my husband, and went back to school, it forced my girls to be more independent. I think it was partially because they saw how much leeway I gave them, and also how strong I was in going on with my life and starting a new career.

Anonymous, mother of two

I just couldn't cope with his anger, I had to seek therapy, go on anti-depressants for a while. I'm finally feeling better. I realize my son is his own person.

Anonymous, mother of one

I had to let go. I tried and tried, but she had all this pent up resentment going back what, twenty years? I finally had to let go.

Anonymous, mother of one

I became more confident when I got divorced and no longer had to take a backseat. I got a degree, a good job in a field I loved. I became a role model. I know the divorce caused them heartache, but because it made me a more rounded, happier person, it did the same for them.

Anonymous, mother of two

One of the boys talks to him, another won't have anything to do with him, and my daughter, no contact either. We're talking thirty-plus years this has been the story. The son who doesn't talk to his father is well within his rights because his father reneged on a business opportunity and that destroyed their relationship. To this day, I do not know why he did that.

Anonymous, mother of three

My boys said, what took you so long? My daughter, nothing — but that's not surprising because we don't talk.

Anonymous, mother of three

Every time my daughter came back from seeing her father, and his second wife, I knew I was in for trouble. The wife filled my daughter with horror stories that I'm sure came from my ex. What was truly disturbing was that my daughter believed them. That was my misery. She was always looking to blame me for the divorce, and whatever they filled her head with, gave her more reason to hate me.

Anonymous, mother of two

It helped that I was a teacher, then a guidance counselor, so I had a background in dealing with kids; nevertheless, I was petrified that my future stepson wouldn't like me. But we bonded right from the first, and that set the stage for going forward and to this day we have a great relationship.

Anonymous, stepmother of one

When children take sides, it's hard to fix problems. I keep looking for ways around it, make it not a 'he said, she said' conversation.

J, mother of two

My second husband-and I have completely different parenting styles. He would let a kid eat off a subway floor and I would make them wash their hands before eating at home. Thankfully, because we are now talking about MY grandchildren, he respects my wishes and says nothing. However, I know he's smiling inside, while I'm fuming.

Anonymous, mother of one

It's always repairable if you talk it out. Sounds simple. Can be harsh. Can make you feel guilty. Can go against your nature.

Anonymous, mother of two

I have repeatedly invited my ex to family functions, but he refuses. He doesn't have the finances he once had and feels ashamed that he can no longer give to his kids. I told him he supported them when they were young, paid for their education so he has nothing to be ashamed of. Because he has gone from a very wealthy man to living day to day, it is very hard for him to see us, or even take any financial help.

Anonymous, mother of three

One of my daughters paid for my wife's divorce lawyer.

Anonymous, father of two

Things did change. Before the divorce, she never criticized me. Now she does. However, my daughter is very polite to my second husband

and never criticizes him. Oh, she says it's now a wonderful parental unit. Can you beat that?

Anonymous, mother of one

One of my daughters resented my second wife for a long time because she had a fantasy about me getting back with her mother.

Anonymous, father of six

Divorce is a bitch. Then, if she's got their ear, the kids wish you would die.

Anonymous, father of three

What do they say, 'happy wife, happy life'. So, if the wife can't appreciate what the husband is doing, not only does it affect the husband, it makes the kids miserable, either by her words or actions. Now that she's my ex, it still carries onto my relationship with my kids.

Anonymous, father of two

Divorce brought the girls and I closer, more together and more of a unit.

Anonymous, mother of two

The one who wanted the most from her father blamed me even though he was very erratic and could never provide the love and attention she needed. The other didn't care and stayed out of it.

Anonymous, mother of two

They know you better than anyone else, and if they detect the slightest tension, they call you on it.

Anonymous, mother of two

> *It's impossible to protect your kids against disappointment in life.*
>
> —Nicholas Sparks, *Message in a Bottle*

Four

Your Marital Status
(Part 2. A Mixed Bag.)

*If nobody teaches you about things
how are you supposed to know about things?*

—P, mother of two

P was speaking about her experience on Tinder and without going into too much detail, let's just say if she had to choose between a very bad hair *year* and Internet dating, she would have chosen the former. What? Your kids never ask? Generally speaking, married kids ask the most questions and a majority of those are prompted by spouses, especially the daughters-in-law. This group seems to be the main culprit. My guess, they're just nosey, and not afraid to either ask directly or push their hubbies to do the interrogation.

Fortunately, P was able to keep a smile on her face and never told her daughter about her misadventures. Other parents talked about the problems of bringing home someone different from Mom or Dad, even though the kids bungee jump or have Chinese tattoo symbols running down their arms. The problem is, they hold us to a higher standard, one that could severely limit our dating choices or force us to do the unthinkable—lead a double life.

Oh, just in case you thought I was leaving out all you parents that are still happily married (whatever number), or in a long-term relationship, remember, no one knows you better than your kids. Your offspring always keep a careful eye on your interactions. If it has always been good, one false look or grimace, directed to your mate, and your kids will immediately pick up on it and worry if the marriage is in trouble. If you've had problems in the past but all is good now, any behavior that reminds them of those problems, can make them extremely anxious and take their fears out on you in angry tirades.

A word to the wise, no matter how innocent, don't call your kids to tell them Dr. Phil is doing this really great show on how married couples lead a double life.

He was never her stepfather. He was her mother's husband.

S, mother of one, stepmother of three

After our divorce, her father revealed personal marital issues that sent her into years of anger directed at me. I didn't know anything about it. I still kick myself for not being a better parent during that time. I was too worried about my own life, being alone for the first time in twenty years was very rough for me.

N, mother of two

Eric Robespierre

My mom always made me feel good. I wanted to share with her. I did the same with my daughter and we were like pals. After I remarried, every time I shared, she turned it around into her thinking I'm somehow questioning her on her behavior. The funny thing is, she loves my second husband. Nothing he says ever offends her.

B, mother of one

I didn't think my son was interested in my marital status until my grandson asked me if I would ever marry another grandpa. I thought that was so cute. He then went on to tell me that his mommy and daddy thought I would so they wouldn't have to take care of me. Can you believe it? Of course, I didn't say anything, but you bet I'm looking at my son differently.

TT, mother of one

My son is always looking out for me. He thinks I'm naïve and will fall for every man who flatters me because they are just after me for my money. I don't want to make him an enemy, but I'm very resentful of the fact he doesn't give me enough credit for choosing men.

V, mother of one

Interested in my life? Not terribly. Children want you to be healthy and happy and not needy.

J, mother of two

My second husband-to-be had three children, a girl and twin boys. When the girl was about to be married, she told my future husband not to bring 'the bitch' to her wedding. I learned later, it was his ex, the mother of his children, who poisoned her and to a lesser degree, the boys against me. It went downhill from there.

Anonymous, mother of one, stepmother of three

After their father died, they became my mother and father. My daughter wants to know whom my date is and where I'm meeting. Are you taking your own car and what time will I be coming home? Very sweet, very solicitous, very interested in my emotional and physical well-being.

S, mother of two

One of my daughters was not ready for me to date, however, she did say that if I found someone who made me happy she would be supportive. My other daughter agreed, together they realized that even though their father had died within the last two years, they just wanted me to be happy and safe. I can't tell you how reassuring that was and how it helped me cope with my husband's passing.

Anonymous, mother of two

Most of my friends say they should have stayed with the father of their children because any new relationship comes with baggage and divorces, when they are messy, can screw up the kids. I can't speak to that because I had a successful marriage and having a great partner made all the difference because you're getting the needed support. Now that he's passed, my kids are still supportive although I don't tell them whom I'm dating and won't unless something serious develops.

Anonymous, mother of two

Regarding my marriage, she brings things up and when appropriate, we discuss it. It's a healthy give and take. Sometimes I will make a point, she will on occasion, say she knows that already, becomes defensive and cuts me off. This is where it becomes tricky and I never go beyond that point.

Anonymous, mother of one

One of my husband's daughters resented me for a long time. I was the evil one. I was the one that broke up the marriage. I think she had a fantasy of him going back to his family. After thirty-one years I gave myself an anniversary gift and stopped talking to her. Almost eleven years later and she made a one hundred and eighty degree turn, and she is very nice to me and I'm nice to her, too.

Anonymous, mother of two

First, I thought she was only jealous of her brother when he was born, but she's been that way with every man that comes into my life, either turning them against me, or just turning away from all of us.

Anonymous, mother of two

I don't tell him anything until it's serious. And then it may not last more than a couple of years. They just have to learn to deal with it. I do. And believe me, it takes more of a toll on me.

Anonymous, mother of one

> *Independence isn't doing your own thing; it's doing the right thing on your own.*
>
> —Kim John Payne

Five

Their Social Life
(Mind Your Own Beeswax.)

*I told her the easiest thing to do was fall in love.
But finding someone you can laugh with...
that's the secret to a lasting marriage.*

—S, mother of two

Ever been called a 'nosy parker'? My interviewees sure have, and if you were to believe them, totally unfairly. They take it as a sign of an ungrateful child who doesn't appreciate that her mother loves them, cares for them and is only looking out for their well-being. Certainly, she is not butting in where she doesn't belong. Certainly, this kindness shouldn't be met with petty squabbles, periods of estrangement or worse, permanent breaks.

Most of all, don't tell them they are in the wrong and their intrusiveness is a sign of their inability to let go and to realize that their kids don't belong to them.

I feebly attempted to assuage their guilt by telling them they were being too hard on themselves. Boy did I read it wrong. They have no guilt!

We Gave Them Life, Now They're Trying To Take Ours

Who am I to question their motives if they want to travel an hour both ways just to check to see if their daughter has made the bed properly?

Listen when they talk. Don't answer until they want your opinion.

P, mother of two

He was always considerate of my feelings. When he was younger and he lived at home he told a girl, who was laying all over him to stop it because his mother didn't like that behavior. Now he stays with us during the summer, has his own room. Maybe that's why he doesn't bring anyone over.

P, mother of two

We talk. I respect them. They are of the modern age. I take their advice on shopping, social media. I take more advice from them than I give.

Anonymous, mother of eight

I'm nosey, so I ask. She's always telling me she's too busy taking care of my granddaughter, or work is occupying most of my time for her to have a social life. She never introduces me to her girlfriends, so I can't question them. Yes, I have thought about asking my granddaughter, but when she was six, I tried that and she told my daughter. I got yelled at. I learned my lesson.

SJ, mother of one

My son has always kept secrets from me so now, even though he lives downstairs and has a wife. I have no idea if he's happy with her or what.

Anonymous, mother of three

We were not judgmental. She was not going to live out my dreams, so her choices are hers.

Anonymous, mother of one

He once showed me a picture of someone he was talking to on social media. She lived in California. I must have made a face, said something—I don't know, but he walked away from me and stopped talking to me for a little while.

P, mother of two

He's 47, doesn't go out to singles bars. He's happy in his solitude. I'm supposed to be happy for him. I feel bad he doesn't go out and look for a relationship. I don't know how he can be happy. I need people. I know I can't be judgmental.

P, mother of two

I want to be their mother. I don't want to be their friend. I want to know what's happening emotionally in their lives. With my son, it takes a long time to breakdown the walls, and once in a while, I'll get a phone call and I'll find out what's happening with him. Once in awhile, I will get to the core, but I never push. It's from my parents. I shared so much with my parents.

Anonymous, mother of two

All they want to do at the moment is vent. They do not want to hear from you. Sure, I shut up, but after a few hours listening to her on the phone, I just have to say—enough.

Anonymous, mother of one

Ok, she's not being open; should be on medication; going to meet someone else in another country. Of course, I'm not thrilled, who would be, but I bite my tongue and let her vent.

Anonymous, mother of one

You could vomit if you knew how many couples have an open relationship where one wants it and another just goes alone with it. My daughter's in one right now and I can tell you it isn't going well.

Anonymous, mother of one

*My mother threw things back in my face.
They were pushy. I sure wasn't going to do the
same when it came to their social life.*

W, mother of three

*He's nearly fifty, but even when he was married he's
always been open and honest with me, asking for
advice, or just telling me about what's going on. I never
ask, always let him bring it. I never criticize, but I do
interject in a friendly way, get him to think things out.*

Anonymous, mother of two

*I learned to keep my mouth shut about her and
her girlfriend. They just get very defensive.
They really don't want your advice.*

Anonymous, mother of two

*When she was serious about someone, and I said
something she thought might be negative, she
responded, "He's family." That made me think
twice and accept what she was saying.*

Anonymous, mother of two

Since she was in high school she hung out with the same kind of kids. All have the same stories, the same substance abuse problems. They gravitated to each other. It was like a sorority. I couldn't control it then, I certainly can't control it now.

Anonymous, mother of three

I have to hear everything she's going through in her life ad nauseam. I tell her, I'm just enabling your craziness if I don't tell you what I think. She listens, tells me what I say does have an impact. Agrees when I'm right. Does she change? Maybe. But I'm her mother and that's what mothers do. They listen. They have a glass of wine after hearing all that stuff.

Anonymous, mother of one

We did talk about one of her relationships. She mentioned he drank too much, said she would talk to him about it. I praised her, told her I hoped it worked out for him. I never brought it up again. I respected her boundaries. I'm never judgmental.

S, mother of two

They both talked to me about dating, about the drama in their lives and that continued up until they got married. I always felt they would figure it out, so I basically only listened.

M, mother of two

It's important to recognize that many times when they tell you about their day, they want you to listen—not to fix things.

Anonymous, mother of two

There is definitely a line of communication, but I know, she is as open as she wants to be.

Anonymous, mother of one

My son had one very good friend that he talked to every few days and had dinner with him when his friend's wife worked late. I thought it was very good for him to socialize, but when he got married, his wife questioned me about that friendship and I got the feeling she was jealous. I suggested she go out with the friend and his wife, get to know them. She said no and that was one of the reasons she cut me out.

Anonymous, mother of two

It started when they were teens. They hid everything, wild reckless things, relationships, drugs and alcohol abuse. I don't know why they never listened to me, my opinions, anything…. I couldn't discipline them. And, I had no backup. Now all I get are drips and drabs, when it suits them, or when I find out from social media.

Anonymous, mother of three

Good people attract good friends.

C, mother of three

Only if I'm asked, so I just talk to them about what's going on. Sure, I'm anxious to know, but I know better than to question them when they don't want to be questioned.

Anonymous, mother of two

The boys, when they need something, they are open with me. One of my daughters has more secrets since she got married. I have to say, she has always been more secretive, and when I hear something about her, I know I have to bail her out. None have an open and honest relationship with their father.

Anonymous, mother of four

Eric Robespierre

You have to be open, meet them where they're at.

J, mother of two

> *They say the apple don't
> fall far from the tree
> but every apple has it own seeds.*
>
> —O. S. Hickman

Six

Your Social Life
(You Have One...?)

My daughter checks the bathroom, my son the bedroom. I'll be damned if I tell them.

—G, mother of two

My children have never asked about my social life and were only supportive when I introduced them to anyone I became seriously involved with. My ex had the same experience, but unfortunately, many of my interviewees haven't been as lucky.

While my findings are limited to my interviews, I did come to certain conclusions. Daughters are usually more interested in their parent's social life and have been known to put their unsuspecting mothers on dating sites. Across the board, sons don't show any curiosity, except if they're married. Their spouse often turns them into amateur sleuths.

All this is very amiable, unless the divorce was ugly and the children were forced to choose sides, or harsher still, totally cut themselves off from one or both parents. This will be a common thread throughout the book; no less important in this section is any new courtship that could actually fracture parental/child relationships beyond repair.

Remember, now that you are dipping your toes into the social scene, when having dinner with the kids, don't mention *Fifty Shades of Grey* and your latest date in the same sentence without risking someone gagging on their food.

What really bothers me about her? She doesn't give me credit for being with someone who has values.

Anonymous, mother of one

I have to accept she will not be a part of my life with him. It is very hurtful.

Anonymous, mother of one

You can't win. Had a thing with my boyfriend. Total misunderstanding, miscommunication and she refuses to see it from his point of view. She crucified him. Put him in a box.

Anonymous, mother of one

My son is very protective. He knew how hard it was for me to lose his father so he doesn't want to see me unhappy again. My two daughters are more optimistic.

They think I should go on a dating site, find somebody because they say I'm still young. I don't feel young.

K, mother of three

If you can't act appropriately in my house when he's here, or his family, I guess I'll see you outside. Guess you won't be attending any events.

Anonymous, mother of one

She has pigeonholed him. She threw back in my face something I said when I didn't really know him too well.

Anonymous, mother of one

I accept her, but not her opinion.

Anonymous, mother of one

They know about my social life, but I don't ask for their advice and they don't give it.

M, mother of two

They are happy I'm doing something— that I have a man in my life.

J, mother of two

Kids have never talked bad about any man that I have dated. On this subject we seem to be on the same page.

Anonymous, mother of two

After their father died they called me once a week, wanted to know what I was doing and that was very touching. However, they both surprised me when they astutely warned me that before I started dating, I shouldn't get involved with someone only because they liked me, but instead, because I liked them! At that point, I realized they understood me better than I understood myself! I don't know when they recognized that someone who adored me, could take me in and that it was important for me to be liked. After I got over the initial shock, I realized what a wonderful gift it was to have such insightful, perceptive children.

Anonymous, mother of two

She has put my boyfriend into a box. Right from the start she has judged him unfairly and now, unfortunately, I can no longer invite her to my house when he's here, or when I have his family over.

Anonymous, mother of one

You're kidding me, right? Kids actually put their parents on a dating site without them knowing it? If my kids did that, I'd die! (Laughter.)

Anonymous, mother of two

> *At age 20, we worry about what others think of us. At age 40, we don't care what they think of us. At age 60, we discover they haven't been thinking of us at all.*
>
> —Ann Landers

Seven

Their Appearance
(Looks Can Kill.)

*I'd tell them when they look like a street urchin,
and they would respect me for that.*

—Anonymous, mother of two

Wow, how is that for having a terrific rapport? Why, I bet if both her forty-year-old kids came straight from the airport after working in Kyoto for two years with Japanese calligraphy running across their foreheads, she'd still get away with saying, "Wash that off before dinner or they'll be no ice cream for you!"

Other parents had negative experiences. One blamed her wealthy paternal grandmother, who threatened to cut off her inheritance if she didn't stop wearing workout pants to Thanksgiving dinner. She now treats her own daughter in a similarly degrading manner. Although, I agreed Doc Martens Pascal Hearts Boots a tad risqué for a fifty-year-old CPA who wants to make partner—*ferme ta bouche* is still the way to let peace reign in providence.

Another realized when she asked her son why he wasn't tucking in his shirt or if baggy pants were still in, that her comments were seen as insensitive and hurting. Consequently it did cause a break in their relationship.

Be warned, if your fifty-year-old shows up with nose rings, don't mention metal detectors, or you may run the risk of her showing you her navel.

She tells me a lot. Not as open with her father. I'm critical of her and she's critical of her children. My mother was critical of me. I think I follow a pattern. Maybe we all do.

P, mother of two

I can't believe you're asking me that because I just had a big problem with my youngest daughter. She got herself a huge tattoo of the Buddha going up her arm. I didn't even know she was into that. Plus, I think it is so unladylike. She calmly explained it was her way of showing him love. I'm afraid I handled it badly and yelled something about him being dead.

Anonymous, mother of two

I'm always thinking— will I make it worse by antagonizing them on this.

Anonymous, mother of two

How do you allow your children to be their own person? Seeing them with nose rings, tattoos at forty, that's the real test. I've failed.

B, mother of one

I weigh every word I say because I never know what is going to annoy him and still I get it wrong…

P, mother of two

I thought as long as you were respectful, you could be honest and open, however, I learned you could mistakenly press one of their FU buttons and then it's like stepping on a landmine.

Anonymous, father of two

They are grown people, and at some point, what we say doesn't register.

B, mother of one

My husband took a backseat to everything. Always wanted the kids to work it out and maybe I was wrong, always fighting with my eldest about her clothing.

Anonymous, mother of two

Never, ever, ever offer any advice. Always assume they are much cleverer than you.

J, mother of two

You should sleep in that shirt, that's how good my son-in-law looks in blue and I told him so. That's how good our relationship is. Of course, if he didn't, I wouldn't say a word.

S, mother of two

You know how moms dress their kids to look good? I didn't do that. You think now, forty-years later I'd change?

Anonymous, mother of two

They think I'm stylish and always compliment me. The same goes for them. They have always had great taste and from their hair to their clothes, always look terrific.

S, mother of two

You always have to acknowledge the whole enchilada. Praise how they look, but then point out where there are opportunities to improve. This works when we talk about dress-down Fridays that can be tricky, when one can look a little too casual.

Anonymous, mother of three

My husband and I were not in sync on this when they were growing up and so nothing has changed now. I will confront them now if I see something isn't right. He lets everything go. I think they appreciate my concern. The difference between when they were kids and now, are how they process what I say. They may get upset at the moment and tell me what's on their mind; there is never any alienation. No, they never acknowledge that what I said had merit. No, thank God, we're not talking about tattoos that cover their entire bodies.

Anonymous, mother of four

Accept their choices even though they are not yours.

T, mother of two

Relationships are always repairable if you think they are.

Anonymous, mother of two

Nose rings, piercing, will bring you to the point of breaking but you must accept him or else lose him.

Anonymous, mother of two

Before he got married he'd ask me if I liked this shirt or those shoes. He's been that way since he was a little boy. Now, I assume he's asking his wife. I found it very endearing, even when he was in his forties.

Anonymous, mother of three

Try not to say anything stupid, which I apparently do all the time.

Anonymous, mother of two

Kids rebel against control. I learned that when they were young and certainly have held to that when they became adults.

Anonymous, mother of two

Don't ever like the way they dress but I would never criticize or say a word. Never gets you anywhere.

Anonymous, mother of two

Always start with a compliment, and then ask your questions.

Anonymous, mother of one

Most advice falls on deaf ears.

Anonymous, mother of two

The first time you see the tattoo of a tiger running across his back, bite your lip until it bleeds if you have to—and for God's sake—do not ask if he intends to put another on his stomach so the first one will have a playmate.

The author, father of two

> *Being an adult means accepting those situations where no action is possible.*
>
> —John D. MacDonald, *The Green Ripper*

Eight

Sibling Rivalry
(One Is Not The Loneliest Number.)

I scolded, I fussed, I didn't put them down when they bickered and they grew out of it.

—Anonymous, mother of two girls

I thought I was in the clear when I followed Erma Bombeck's advice when she wrote, "It goes without saying that you should never have more children than you have car windows."

Two kids, two side windows—all good, right? Wrong! It wasn't until they were into their thirties I discovered who was responsible for the backseat commotion causing me to go apoplectic and threaten to pull over to make even more pathetic threats. (Like, I was going to abandon them in the snowy woods…?)

I believe their rivalry never went beyond those trivial incidents that didn't last past their adolescence because, beneath it all, they had a loving relationship that has grown deeper as both married and had families of their own.

My interviews record similar stories of good fortune, however, there were too many stories of how sibling rivalry had torn apart families, bringing many of my interviewees to tears.

For those of you who have similar tales of woe, be strong and take heart. Remember, you are still the parent, so at the very least avoid stroking the flames of discord. Don't take sides and keep your individual relationships as loving and positive as you can.

Finally, stop telling everyone on Facebook you only have one child, the doctor. Most parents would love to have a ski instructor in the family.

I have three, (pause, laughs) yeah, I have three of them and they are all quite different but they all get along.

Anonymous, mother of three

She is a wonderful sister and he is a terrific brother. He worries about her, her children. Whenever she needs them to be taken somewhere, or picked up, he'll make himself available. He drives them to school. I think since she got divorced, and that was over ten years ago, he's been even more supportive.

P, mother of two

From the time they were born they were different, but never rivals. She was amazing, never a problem right up to her teens. He fought me on everything and because he was very articulate, won every argument. Funny, he never had a problem with her.

Anonymous, mother of two

My son and daughter get along when they see each other, which is not very often. I wish they had a better relationship, but thanks to his wife they don't.

N, mother of two

She was jealous of him from the very first moment I was pregnant. Even asked me why I wanted another child. I thought she would grow out of it. Boy, was I wrong.

Anonymous, mother of two

You ask him, I favored her. You ask her, I favored him.

Anonymous, mother of two

My daughter got so upset when she saw how her brother treated me after my husband died that she told him she never wanted to have anything to do with him anymore. She never even mentions her brother to her own children. Sure, my fragile health and breaking his promise to take care of me after their father died set her off.

Anonymous, mother of two

My son was jealous of his sister the moment she took her first breath. Was that the reason he had a hand in getting her onto drugs?

Anonymous, mother of three

He had a very serious, near-death experience as a child that probably is the cause of his hypochondria. It is only good fortune for him that his sister is a doctor and can give him sound medical advice that reassures and calms him down. I think that relationship wouldn't work if they hadn't been caring and supportive of each other from the time they were young with never a hint of sibling rivalry.

Anonymous, mother of two

There was never any rivalry, which was surprising, because I gave one much more attention than the other two, but no jealously ever occurred because of that. I've thought of talking to them about it, but my husband warned me not to upset the applecart.

Anonymous, mother of three

She and my son are so different. He's more like me, quiet, not much of a risk-taker. She's an adventurist. Had a motorcycle. That's where all my grey hair comes from. She takes after her father, he after me. I don't think it effects their relationship, at least they never bring it up with me, tells me their personalities is what keeps them from being closer.

N, mother of two

It's no use. As soon as she finds out one of our kids screwed up, she starts comparing them to the ones that don't. No wonder they don't want to talk to their mother.

Anonymous, father of four

It was his wife that caused all the trouble. I've been very sick, all sorts of serious problems. I nearly died a few times. When my husband passed my son said not to worry, he'd take time off from his job, find a way to take me into the city to see my doctors. I don't drive. All that changed when he got married. She became very jealous. She even got between him and his best friend so they don't even see each other anymore. My daughter got very upset. Read him the riot act. Now they don't talk. They were close growing up. That's all forgotten now, thanks to his wife.

Anonymous, mother of two

Why is it always the same? One child resents the other for being born, yet the child, who is resented, idolizes the other—always to no avail.

Anonymous, mother of two

Eric Robespierre

I think having children too close together can be harmful to their growth because you can't give each one the attention they deserve. But, you know what—that never caused problems with her siblings, only with me.

Anonymous, mother of four

I don't know if this is as much sibling rivalry as a difference in their realities. They just see their father's death, and my handling of it, in opposite ways. Causes friction between them. Before that I can say there wasn't much sibling rivalry.

Anonymous, mother of two

I have always dealt with them differently, as two separate individuals, and perhaps that's why, they were never rivals.

M, mother of two

It's no question in my daughter's mind I love my son more than her. Of course, it's absurd.

M, mother of two

Sometimes, I think I'm like a baseball umpire running into the middle of a fracas and getting trampled to the ground.

Anonymous, father of three

They never liked each other. Each of them is selfish and none cares about the other. It just got worse over the years. It happened before my divorce so that's not the cause. I have no idea why.

Anonymous, father of three

They were rivals since always and I don't think it will ever end. My mom was ninety and her sister eighty-eight and they still had a sibling rivalry.

Anonymous, mother of two

I think because one was social and the other an introvert, there was never any rivalry and they accepted each other's differences. Funny, because I'm very social, I had trouble with my son and had to learn to accept him; whereas his sister, the one who I like to say dodged the raindrops, was just like me.

Anonymous, mother of two

They could have achieved more had they not shortchanged each other in their separate individualities. Did I have something to do with it? Who knows?

Anonymous, mother of three

The biggest problem, they grew up not having any meaningful relationship. Any interaction they had, had to do with the older one trying to control the younger sibling. She never remembered what it was like to be his age. There was never any kindness, certainly not any love on the older one's part, and the younger finally got tired of being talked down to and being rejected.

Anonymous, mother of two

She would be talking about her work, something or other, and suddenly she'd bring up the subject of her brother, always accusing me of defending him when they were growing up. Or, giving him all the attention. Believe me, nothing I can say will convince her otherwise. We're not speaking anymore.

Anonymous, mother of two

My daughter screamed a lot at her brother. She would say things to him that were so obnoxious. I tried to correct her behavior, but I was never able to get through to her, make her more respectful and certainly couldn't make her care, or love him. I hoped that would change, kept trying to mend fences until she broke off all relationship with me. Fortunately, my son has made peace with it. It still breaks my heart.

Anonymous, mother of two

There was never any rivalry. They just don't talk. Maybe because she is a part of my life and he isn't? She worries about me, he doesn't. Maybe she is angry with him for that?

Anonymous, mother of two

I was put in an orphanage along with one sister. My brother stayed with my mother and now we're pretty close. I tried to make sure my kids stayed close, but when one doesn't like another one, for no reason, you can tell them all the stories of your life and it won't make a difference.

Anonymous, mother of three

They were rivals from the beginning. The boys fought with each other and I never interfered. The girls were all into sports and never had much to do with each other.

Anonymous, mother of eight

I only have one child, but it's my sibling rivalry that has caused a disagreement with my own daughter. She wants me to have a relationship with my sister. She sees her as the unstable one and I should be the good sister. Unless it's a family occasion, I want nothing to do with her. No fucking way I'm going to put myself

*out there for her. Maybe you'll put this in your book?
I'm sure I'm not the only one who has this problem.*

Anonymous, mother of one

I have a twin sister who has always been jealous of me. Nevertheless, I tried to be a good sister. I gave her a job and she stole from me. I haven't spoken with her in over twenty-five years. Unfortunately, my daughter and she are close and because my sister is always bad-mouthing me, my daughter and I have problems. It gets worse. When my sister stole from me, my son cut off all contact with his aunt, but because his sister hasn't, he won't talk to her until she does the same.

Anonymous, mother of two

*One always tried to top the other.
Personality differences I guess.*

Anonymous, mother of three

Never had any problems. I had them follow rules and they were all fair to each other. They always liked each other, took care to watch over each other. The boys were involved in sports and played together. I tried to make everything equal because I'm a Libra.

Anonymous, mother of three

One of the twins, my daughter, will not speak to her non-twin brother while the brothers do speak. I have never gotten an answer except it goes deep and started when she was fourteen. The boys have no idea why, either. It is something I have to accept, along with a lot of other types of behavior that upset me.

Anonymous, mother of three

I think, when you have kids, even when they are twins, there are no clear answers to why some bond and others do not. Nature vs. nurture? Well, that question always comes up when you ask yourself, why do your children behave the way they do? For me, the most rational explanation—it's a combination—of course—to what degree can often tip the scales.

Anonymous, mother of two

One child was private, the other, like me, outgoing and shared the sense of the ridiculous, but that never caused any rivalry and they were very close. However, it does cause problems with me, because I'm more comfortable with him.

Anonymous, mother of two

Eric Robespierre

> *My mom says I'm her sugarplum.*
> *My mom says I'm her lamb.*
> *My mom says I'm completely perfect.*
> *Just the way I am.*
> *My mom says I'm a super-*
> *special wonderful little guy.*
> *My mom just had another baby.*
> *Why?*
>
> —Judith Viorst

Nine

Non-Biological
(Same As It Ever Is.)

Everything depends on upbringing.

—Leo Tolstoy, *War and Peace*

Because this chapter is about how parents deal with their non-biological children, I thought I'd ask my interviewees if they agreed with Mr. Tolstoy. While I interviewed a fair number of stepparents, I was only able to interview one mother who adopted, however, there was a silver lining—she did it twice!

This extraordinary woman, who wishes to stay anonymous, tells of a journey to a foreign land, so perilous, so traumatic that at times frustration and despair nearly overwhelmed her and her husband. Despite the obstacles and setbacks, they never gave up hope, and eventually their dreams of having a child were granted, *twice over*. If this stressful ordeal wasn't enough for one human being to endure, simultaneously, she had to deal with numerous life-threatening illnesses that continue to endanger her life.

I'm not telling you this to get your sympathy, but to give you some perspective and insight into her situation. As soon as she and her husband felt the children could understand what it meant to be adopted, she, carefully and lovingly, told them the truth. She didn't go into the harrowing details, nor did she say anything negative about their biological parents. Instead, she focused on the positive. She picked bedtime when they usually were most receptive. She explained, as gently as she could, that they were special and that she and her husband chose them for that reason.

Both children calmly accepted the situation. As they grew to adulthood, nothing changed their attitude. Neither chose to search for their biological mothers; instead, became even closer to her, whom they loved as if she was their natural mom.

When I asked her where she came out on the Nature vs. Nurture issue, she laughed. As far as personality traits, since she didn't know the real parents, she couldn't provide any insight on how nature played a part. As far as nurture was concerned, she and her husband gave them all the love, comfort and security they could, but when it was all said and done, she smiled and told me she believed luck played the most important part in how they turned out. I had to laugh. All of my interviewees, regardless of the topic, always mentioned luck in one way or another.

When her children grew to adulthood, she had more than the 'luck issue' in common with the other parents. Her problems ticked off all the same boxes. A jealous daughter-in-law tries to breakup the mother and son relationship. The son now cannot fulfill his promise of taking mom to her doctor appointments. His sister takes up the slack, accuses him of betraying their mom in favor of his new wife and consequently, cuts off all communication with him.

I'm disappointed I haven't been able to gather more responses, however, my guess is that regardless of biology, we're all in the same boat when it comes to figuring out how to avoid going sideways when we communicate with our children as adults. As to Nature vs. Nurture, I say… luck be a lady tonight!

Finally, no more fibbing! Sure, back in the day you could lie and tell them how lucky they were to have been adopted by pillars of the community. Now, with YouTube, the world knows grandpa's in jail for installing hidden cameras in Victoria Secret dressing rooms and Mom likes to do a striptease after shooting par at the country club.

One of my grandsons was adopted. Of mixed race, but always seemed comfortable with whites. Black Lives matter put him at odds with my political views. When he became disrespectful, I had to end our relationship. Probably will never see him again.

Anonymous, mother of four

It's a crapshoot, but then what isn't?

Anonymous, father of three

I decided from the start, I wouldn't be the disciplinarian. That was his father's job. I'd step back let his dad set the parameters. That's not to say my husband

and I wouldn't discuss things, or when things got a little bumpy, I'd intercede without first telling him.

Anonymous, stepmother of one

He never got in trouble in school when he was young. I was like that, so maybe he got that from me. Then I found out he sat so still in his seat because he was embarrassed because he couldn't follow what was going on. Sitting that way also gave him so much stress he came home with headaches. We took him to a doctor and found out he had attention deficit. That must have been inherited, but the combination of medication, therapy and tutoring got him through public school and college, and now he has a great job and is very successful.

Anonymous, mother of three

At first I wasn't as supportive, but later I thought about what she said—what I said… and I agreed that perhaps I wasn't as open-minded. Now, I love him like I do my other grandchildren. My daughter knows that. I don't think she holds it against me.

Anonymous, mother of five

It takes more than one person to raise a child, and my two adopted children had an extended family that loved them. Their grandparents made them feel loved and accepted from the very moment they joined our family. That was so important in their development.

M, mother of two

It's a big difference if it's not your biological child. You can distance yourself. Not be as critical.

Anonymous, stepmother of three

I made up my mind that they needed time to themselves and even now that he's a grown man with his own family, I make sure that when we visit him I insist that he and his father have time alone.

Anonymous, stepmother of one

I find myself being overly cautious with my adoptive son, but not so much with my other boy. My husband points this out to me. He tells me I shouldn't be that way since both boys, now in their forties, have always shown me the same amount of love, affection and grief. He says I should do the same. I will try. Oh, I should add, he never had that problem.

Anonymous, mother of two

As soon as they could look at picture books I made sure they saw the word adopted, so they knew the word before they knew what it meant. I thought I could ease them into its meaning. They were both okay with it, until my daughter was a teen when, out of the blue, she wanted to know if she was a pretty baby, a good baby? When I answered she was, she dropped the bombshell and asked, 'then why did her mother give her up?' When I said she loved her so much she brought her to X, so they could find her a family that could raise her and give her all the love she deserved. From that moment on, there was not another word on the subject. I think that moment of honesty strengthened the bond we already had and it has never weakened, some forty years later.

Anonymous, mother of two

As they grow, they learn they can trust you, depend on you, that you're always there. I think this is important for all children, but especially for those adopted.

M, mother of two

Honestly, I really don't know if I would ever do it again, or tell someone not to do it. I'm smart enough to know it's the luck of the draw, and who am I to tell someone it won't be them that are the lucky ones.

Anonymous, mother of two

My daughter found her birth mom, wrote to her, but the birth mom wrote back, don't ever contact me again. I don't want to speak to you, or ever have anything to do with you, or for you to have anything to do with my children, grandchildren, because you will destroy their lives. She was very harsh and it was upsetting to my daughter. It's like she gave up on my daughter twice.

Anonymous, mother of two

My kids sat me down, and said if I get divorced again, they wanted to go with him. His kids got a kick out of that. Never sure what they meant by that. (She giggles)

Anonymous, stepmother of three

I think circumstance can create the problems between siblings, not just ones that are adopted. They were never close, but they were always friends, until she saw how he treated me and that was the end of their relationship. Who knows, maybe she was always harboring some kind of anger toward him? What's horrible is her children will grow up without knowing her brother and his family.

Anonymous, mother of two

I look at them as individuals, hers and mine, everyone based on their value systems.

Anonymous, stepfather of three

When my first child was in kindergarten, he asked me for five dollars. I wanted to know why he needed five dollars and he said there was a boy on the bus who, for five dollars, would get him to meet his real mother. I told him to tell the boy I was his real mother and that was that. I also called the principal who said we have an extortionist in kindergarten! (She laughed)

Anonymous, mother of two

My son-in-law got my daughter a gift certificate to Ancestry.com and she called me and told me about the idea of looking for her birth mother, and said if I was against it, she wouldn't do it. I said, you have the right, she has the right, just don't call her mom. She said that would never happen because you are my mom.

Anonymous, mother of two

Only having two adopted children, I cannot compare to having my own, however, based on friends and relatives, relationships, good and bad, have no boundaries.

Anonymous, mother of two

I adopted my husband's children, included them in the process. She was my maid of honor and he was my husband's best man. My daughter is my best friend and she, I. I am also very close with my son. I was determined.

Anonymous, mother of two

I told my son there was a form he could fill out and he could find his birth mom. He said, unless they are famous, or rich, I don't need to get in touch with them. He's always been like that; you know... what's in it for me. My daughter, on the other hand, is more sentimental, more emotional and that's why I was worried about how she would take her birth mother's rejection, but she seems to be fine.

Anonymous, mother of two

It was a niece of the birth mother who contacted my daughter, and said, if you want, I can put you in contact with your five sisters and brothers, or your twenty nieces and nephews. My daughter asked my advice, and we both thought it wasn't a good idea to go against the birth mother's wishes so she doesn't contact them.

Anonymous, mother of two

> *Superman was adopted.*
>
> —The author

Ten

The Grandchildren
(Want to see their Facebook Page?)

*Gone are the days of carrying a photo
of a grandkid in your wallet.*

—Anonymous, father of three

One anonymous father resisted as long as he could, but finally loaded up his iPhone with pictures his kids sent, and dutifully scrolled through as many as he could before the viewer's eyes rolled back in their heads. It wasn't his idea. It was his wife, who relied on all things technological.

It was ironic, he said, because back in the day, his wife never carried any photos of their kids, and if it weren't for the ones he had in his wallet, they never would have had any to show friends.

Laugh if you want to, but with social media playing such an important role in promoting one's personae, grandparents are going to the extreme. Take for instance, the parent who posted her daughter's sonogram photos on Facebook, or the father who told me he was putting together a LinkedIn page for his infant grandson in order to impress the admissions director at an exclusive nursery school.

However, this was the response I heard most often, "I like my grandkids more than my kids because I can leave their home anytime I want."

Nevertheless, there was an undercurrent of braggadocio that pointed an unflattering portrait of some of my parents who fit the 'stage mother' profile to a T.

Unfortunately, their unbridled bluster caused me guilt because I have never trumpeted my own grandchildren's grandiosity. Not one gushing utterance of their brilliance, virtuosity, or Hollywood good looks. Not even the slightest exaggeration, or blatant untruth, even if I do believe my two-year-old, drummer-granddaughter, is the second coming of Sheila E., and my grandsons will be building robots at MIT before they're fifteen.

I used to think my outlier attitude was the result of my disappointment in seeing that the kids don't look like me, but I came to my senses by watching Dr. Phil who made it clear that paternity tests can cause more harm than good.

Alright, I'm being half-way disingenuous, but I believe being an outlier has allowed me to sidestep some of the obvious pitfalls, perhaps allowing for an harmonious relationship, contrasting with my over-enthusiastic interviewees who confessed their actions have often set their own relationships on fire.

Take for example, the attitude that love means always spoiling them rotten. Oh, and don't think just because you tell them to keep it a secret, your kids won't know who bought their sixteen-year-old a Corvette for their high school graduation.

Finally let me leave you with these helpful hints:

1. Never buy grandkids burner phones so you can keep your communications secret.
2. Don't secretly take them to a plastic surgeon because you want them to look more like you, than the in-laws.
3. When babysitting, if you're planning on taking them to Disney World, leave a note.

The way they helicopter them, much of that interference I disagree with. I wonder if they do it as a reaction to our parenting them?

Anonymous, father of six

I see my downfalls and am aware of them, but I was taught you wash your hands when you come in from the street.

B, mother of one

The problem is my perspective reality. It becomes difficult when your child raises their child in a different way, one you wouldn't agree with. It's very hard not to butt in, did it early on with my daughter. Slight disagreements we eventually ironed out. I stopped completely. Never with my son's kids. I have a wonderful daughter-in-law and I know better. That's how you keep a good relationship.

Anonymous, mother of two

I was never involved in the minutiae. They were always good at figuring out what to do and that goes for the grandkids.

          M, mother of two

You want to be helpful. You're older, you lived through it and you think maybe your advice can be useful. I never give it to be critical. I don't want to make trouble. Unfortunately, they don't always take it that way, in the spirit in which you give it.

        Anonymous, mother of two

Time out? To me, time out was you better run to your room before I kill you.

          J, mother of six

I have sixteen grandchildren. Most I keep in touch with—some not so much. I text them once a week and they text me back. My kids love that I do it.

        Anonymous, mother of eight

She came up to me during a holiday event and said she felt sad. I asked why, but she told me she didn't know. She's thirteen and I figured it had to do with her mother being unhappy. I will listen forever, but she didn't want to talk anymore and I won't bring anything up about the divorce.

Anonymous, mother of one

Your kids are one half you, your grandkids are one quarter you— three quarters are total strangers.

Anonymous, mother of two

I do a lot of observation. Ninety-nine percent of the time I keep my mouth shut. If I'm forced to, I do it gingerly, but even then, I can be shot down. The bottom line, if you start to interfere, your relationship will go down the tubes.

M, mother of two

My granddaughter got a job at a local ice cream parlor so my daughter took me there. I made the remark that I hope she doesn't like her job too much. She got on me. It was a stupid thing to say. Same type of demeaning stuff my mother would say to me. No, that behavior is something I should not have carried on to my grandchildren.

Anonymous, mother of two

One of my grandkids has very bad manners, so I sent a book on manners to my daughter, rather than my granddaughter. I told her, this is a book she should have, but I'm giving it to you, so you can decide what to do. She said she'd think about it. I believe you should never directly confront your grandchild because that's the parent's job. One of my in-laws circumvented the parent, directly went to the child and caused a great deal of animosity in the family.

Anonymous, father of six

I never told my granddaughter about her mother's drug problems. Just said she was travelling a lot. She's been with me now for five years. My daughter's been sober for three. They see each other. I have five others from my son. They're always around because he lives downstairs. I see them all the time and I love it. I never complain to their father about their behavior. It's a two-family house. Just creates problems, because he'd punish them.

Anonymous, mother of three

I went to my eldest grandson's baseball game. It was a big deal. I don't remember why. But I always go. I had to put up with my ex son-in-law who is the biggest moron to walk the face of the earth. But I was really polite. I'm always polite. You have to be. He's his father.

Anonymous, mother of three

Disagree with the way they are disciplining their kids… only thing to do is curl up in a ball and wait until the churning in your stomach stops.

J, mother of six

Eric Robespierre

They live six hours away and we Facetime with our eight-year-old grandson every weekend. What's also great is my stepson, his wife they always get into the conversation so it becomes a family affair.

Anonymous, stepmother of one

My husband couldn't take the noise. Not saying it was the reason he left. I don't have any problems. They dirty up the place. I clean it when they leave. My mother couldn't take the noise either. Maybe three, maybe eight, with all of them here, doesn't bother me. Sometimes their mothers come over. I used to have problem with two of them, but it's ok now. And their mothers... Oh, my god! Sometimes they're worse than the wives, but after all these years, it's much better.

Anonymous, mother of three

They are fabulous to us. They are extraordinarily polite, respectful and loving in every possible way. My only problem, and I stress mine, because my wife isn't as bothered as I am, that they are not interested in social issues. They give us some dumbass excuse, which pisses me off even more. The ironic thing, their parents march. Don't get me started. I'm pissed at them because they let them get away with it. I would not have let them get away with it. They're coddled. It's also a lack of education. They have no concept of what our government is all about. Their whole life is consumed with getting the next iPhone or what's on Instagram or YouTube.

Anonymous, father of six

I'm a better grandmother than mother. (Giggles.)

Anonymous, mother of two

I didn't want to go a party for an eight-year-old, running around the park shooting paint guns at each other, but my daughter tells me he wanted me to come. How could I refuse?

Anonymous, mother of two

When we take the grandkids out to eat I say, eat whatever you want, but my wife says no, we have more traditional values.

Anonymous, father of three

When they are with me, what they eat is an issue. Stuff yourself with bread and soda and of course you don't have an appetite. If we are with their parents, I don't say anything.

Anonymous, mother of three

I asked about my granddaughter, who is in college, because I wanted to know if she was still seeing her boyfriend. Right away my daughter became confrontational. She sets out boundaries and said, 'Ask her, don't ask me'. Why so confrontational? Apparently, my granddaughter accused her mother of telling Nana (that's me) everything, so now my daughter doesn't want to get in trouble.

Anonymous, mother of three

I always say there is room for me to improve and now my grandson repeats it back to me. (Laughs.)

Anonymous, mother of one

We need to come around and accept our differences. My grandson is dating an Asian young lady. Times have changed and we have to embrace change with love and understanding.

Anonymous, mother of two

In a perfect world, I should have done what my husband said to do and give them anything they want. They are not going to faint from having that soda, but that's not me. I have to say something, that's my personality.

Anonymous, mother of three

I make subtle hints about what they can, and cannot, eat and they never give me any trouble. I check with the parents first, make sure they give me leverage. I want to make sure they eat healthy, but every so often, the kids have to be themselves.

Anonymous, mother of two

They are out of the box. When you live in a retirement community and they come to visit without their parents, it adds another component to your life.

Anonymous, father of six

I can't take care of three young children anymore. Don't know what's wrong with me? Guess I'm not a spring chicken anymore. I was exhausted. Not only physically, but mentally. Always something they wanted, they needed, or they didn't have. Not a minute to yourself.

Anonymous, mother of one

She did a number on my grandchildren. One is in college, the other two, still in high school. I am reestablishing a relationship with the older one, but he still seems to be under his mother's influence, as is his brother. I'm not sure they will ever be part of their extended family because she made the divorce so difficult for everyone.

Anonymous, mother of two

I came from a culture where anyone in the family could discipline the children. It was consistent. You had to be polite to your friends, family, relatives, all adults. You had to have good table manners. Now, I can't say boo to my grandkids, or mention their behavior to my daughter, or son-in-law. They don't want my advice. They would only take it as a criticism of their abilities.

Anonymous, mother of one

I don't go out of my way, but when their behavior is extreme and I don't find it acceptable, I do feel compelled to talk to my children about their children. I try to do it in a way nobody gets defensive. It's all about feeling comfortable—me— my kids.

Anonymous, father of three

They are cautious around me. I can read their body language. They're leery of me. This is what happens when my soon to be ex and my kids talk bad about me, in front of my grandkids.

Anonymous, father of two

I don't see my grandchildren enough to recognize their relationship with their parents or me, so I button-up when I see them. Plus, it becomes

*even more complicated depending on how good
your relationship is with your own kids.*

Anonymous, mother of three

*My grandson is autistic, and I send my son articles about
the subject, and info from friends in similar situations
and it is the one thing that brings us closer together.
I just wish it were under better circumstances.*

Anonymous, mother of two

*I can't help it, maybe it's because they have to be told
to hug me, call me Pop-Pop, or some stupid name
I had no part in choosing, but I don't feel as close
to them as I do my own kids. I keep that to myself
when my friends go on and on about their grandkids
like they walk on water or something. I don't want
them to think there is something wrong with me.*

Anonymous, father of three

*In order to have a better and closer relationship with
my grandchildren I decided to learn what they learn.
I ask them to teach me what they know. When people
are allowed to talk to each other, and have common
interests, that makes for a stronger relationship.*

Anonymous, mother of one

Eric Robespierre

Because I live out of the country and come in two or three times a year, I don't fit in with my daughter's family. I'm not part of their ensemble, if you know what I mean? Not involved in the day-to-day life, in that loop—just a visitor. Grandparents become less useful. You have to be very brave to grow old, don't you think?

Anonymous, mother of two

> *They say genes skip a generation. Maybe that's why grandparents find their grandchildren so likable.*
>
> —Joan McIntosh

Eleven

Distance Makes The Heart Grow Sadder
(Or Does It?)

When they're out into the world, making their own income, living on their own, you have to let go.

—Anonymous, mother of two

Let's face it—for many of us, two steps to a hug are about the longest distance we'd like to travel when it comes to seeing our adult children.

Remember the film, *The Good, The Bad and The Ugly*? Remember your skin prickling and the feeling you got as that eerie whistling dramatized the coming confrontation between Clint Eastwood, Lee Van Cleef and Eli Wallach? Well, that's the sensation I felt as my interviewees began to tell me about how they felt when their kids settled far from home.

The 'good' brought compelling, lucrative job opportunities, or an adventurous lifestyle many parents wished they hadn't passed up. The 'bad' usually had to do with running away from something, or running to something, that didn't hold much hope for success. The 'ugly' was just that. A rift in the parent-adult child relationship so deep, no forwarding address was given leaving them in total darkness as to the health and happiness of their progenies.

It's obvious the last two categories bring heartache and longing, but even when kids are flourishing to the point of paying for their parents to fly half-way across the US to see them at holiday time, it's tough to get used to the fact they can't hug and kiss their kids every Friday night, or drop over to watch the grandkids play Little League.

I was surprised my interviewees were mature enough to recognize that, hard as it may have been to let go (and still may be), their kids don't belong to them, and that they had to give them the space they required to blossom as adults. I was even more taken aback by parents who have steeled themselves to the fact they may never see their kids (or grandkids) ever again, yet continue to hope and pray that at the very least, lines of communications will once more open up.

Some last thoughts. Never put tracking devices on them when they turn eighteen, even though it works great for pets. And never ask Interpol to find them because you didn't pack their suitcase and you're afraid they won't have enough clean underwear.

My husband gets on the phone and he doesn't want to create waves so he placates them. He zips it. I argue, confront, defend, and of course, listen. It can be hurtful when they hang up. It can be harmful because we yell.

But it can be extremely helpful when the next day, or week, we talk it out and come to an understanding. Because they live far away, this is the only way we have any meaningful relationship. At least for our family.

Anonymous, mother of two

It breaks my heart I can't jump into the car and drive over to his house, but what can I do? She got a job in Seattle. He had to go. She makes twice what he does. He eventually found something, but I'm not sure he's as happy as he was here in New York. Thank God, my husband and I can get on a plane and go out there for the holidays. Still, it's not the same thing.

HK, mother of one

We're closer to some because they live nearer. That's just the reality.

J, mother of six

Whenever I talk to her, I always sound excited. Even if I haven't heard from her in a very long time I never ask why, yet somehow she always thinks I'm accusing her of something. I don't know, maybe I just don't know how to talk to her?

B, mother of one

My son lives out of state, so I don't see him as often as I'd like. I try to talk to him once a week, but because of his wife we can only speak in generalities and sometimes more than a week goes by. Fortunately, my daughter lives close by so I see her on the weekends. That makes up for it, I guess.

N, mother of two

They all live elsewhere. They all are different, but in that they're the same. I'm not happy about that, but that's their choice.

Anonymous, mother of four

I was fine with them moving away. It was what they wanted. I'm not going to live their lives. I'll see them when I can. And you know what, when he sees a great airfare, he buys me a ticket and I'm there the next day.

Anonymous, mother of two

My daughter felt guilty she left me all by myself in _____ and moved to America. I was happy she was independent and did what she needed to do.

J, mother of two

I don't live anywhere close to them, and I feel I'm not part of their lives, their structure… I'm not needed.

Anonymous, mother of two

My son got divorced and had full custody of his young son, unfortunately, he lives far away from me and any other family member, and he had to put my grandson into daycare. My husband and I felt powerless.

Anonymous, mother of three

Animals in the animal kingdom need to let go of their children at a certain age.

J, mother of two

I just called my son in San Diego and asked how the weather was. He said it's been the most humid summer he could remember. I told him I might not come. I don't know why I said that. I feel guilty. I think I'll call him back, tell him I was only kidding.

Anonymous, mother of three

Distance is certainly a factor, but between the kids having jobs, the grandkids having class trips, after-school activities, summer camps, it makes them coming to us virtually impossible. Then, when we visit, there is such a small window during which we can spend any quality time with any of them.

B, father of five

Naturally, I'm sorry they don't live closer so I could see them and my grandchildren on a regular basis, but my goal was to raise them as independent people because I wasn't, and I saw how important that characteristic was to being a happy and mature person.

Anonymous, mother of two

Both my kids live far away, and of course, I would like them to live closer, but this is 2018 and it is always about the jobs… where they can make their living. My husband and I need to accept their life.

Anonymous, mother of two

He's halfway across the country. I don't see him. I email him every day, some nice quote and a little note to tell him what I'm doing. I'm trying to get him interested in my life. He never answers. I'm typing a relationship into the wind.

Anonymous, mother of one

I don't see them often enough, so when I do, I want to catch up. That means no small talk, and when you narrow it down to just the important stuff, it may be too much for them. Communication is important, but to be effective, it has to be consistent. If they don't get to know you, you don't get to know them.

Anonymous, father of two

If you give them an open invitation to come and bring the kids, especially when it's the summer and I have the pool and the beach, I am not going to call every weekend and beg them. And, when I hear they visit friends in a nearby town and only come by me to take a shower by the pool, it hurts.

Anonymous, father of two

It's a lifelong process, communicating with your kids and distance can make it more difficult, but not impossible.

Anonymous, mother of two

I don't buy it. My daughter would still show her concern, and my son would still never call or email me. I know this because my daughter travels to Europe and my son lives a few miles away.

Anonymous, mother of two

They both live out of state and I don't see them much, but that's ok. They have a life and that's the way it should be. I don't let that get in the way of

Eric Robespierre

*our communicating with each other, when we can,
nor the amount of love I have for them both.*

Anonymous, mother of two

*I feel I don't have a family anymore. They
live in America and I live in ___.*

Anonymous, mother of two

*Family, like branches on a tree,
we all grow in different directions,
yet, our roots all remain as one.*

—Anonymous

Twelve

Downsizing
(The Up Side.)

*We all agreed memories aren't in the house,
they're in our heads.*

—S, mother of two

I put this quote at the top of this section because it provided a ray of sunshine in an otherwise bleaker picture.

For example, one mother told me if she had known that selling her house would be such a problem, she would have burned it down. Going to jail, she said would have been a lot less heartbreaking. She was joking, but I know many a truth is said in jest.

There may be no way to avoid such angst, however, to lessen its impact, parents can start by being as honest and forthright about their needs, including the state of their own finances. They must also be sensitive to how unsettling it can be for their kids, and how a family sits down, addressing their apprehension will help in alleviating the anxiety.

A thought. Even if the kids were all for downsizing, buying a camper and parking it in their driveway might not be what they had in mind.

Finally, ask the kids if they don't mind you including their sleds in any lawn sale. You don't want them mouthing the words 'Rose Bud' on their deathbed.

Let's face it, they couldn't afford it and we were in no position to just give them the house outright. They knew we needed the money to buy the place in Georgia. I can't understand why they accused us of being selfish and won't see us anymore.

Anonymous, father of two

I didn't tell them. I knew they couldn't afford to buy it and I didn't want them going into debt.

S, mother of one

There are boundaries. Once you are out of the house, our downsizing is one you don't cross. However, I could never let it get to the point where I wouldn't say, let me hear your story.

Anonymous, mother of two

The way she blew up, it came out of the blue. When she was a kid she hated the neighborhood. Couldn't wait to go halfway around the country to college. When she moved back, she didn't come home, moved into the city, got married, moaned and groaned every time she came back for holiday meals because the burbs were so boring. Now, when the house just got too much for us and we decided to downsize, get a place in Manhattan, she wants us to give her the house. She and her husband are thinking of starting a family and living here would be just perfect.

Anonymous, mother of one

I was all set to sell the house to my eldest daughter who has two kids and is definitely outgrowing her own home when my youngest, who isn't married, has no kids and never mentioned she wanted to put family over her career, went bonkers. She accused me (she's daddy's little girl and wouldn't say boo to him, even though he was in favor of selling the house to J), of favoritism, loving J more than I loved her. She even threatened to take us to court (she's an attorney), but thank God that never happened. It caused such a rift that she and her sister still are not talking. Me, she hates with a passion.

Anonymous, mother of two

One of my daughters had some emotional minutes, but they were sweet moments.

S, mother of two

Major problem. Like I told you before, I mentioned it to him but he never took it seriously. Like everything else in his life. Now, I don't know. He may be doing what I'm doing… buying a mobile home. I don't really know, but he better do something quick because I can't take him in. I can't be giving him any more money. He's got a decent job.

Anonymous, mother of three

I'm going to be very careful when I tell my children. More calculating. Learned from my years of handling them that they are all going to have different reactions and I'm going to have to deal with each of them. Sometimes, I think we should have kids in our sixties and seventies. (Laughs). I don't mean physically. I mean emotionally.

H, mother of three

They called me an organized hoarder. First laugh I had after my husband died and we all decided the best thing to do was for me to sell.

Anonymous, mother of two

Kids sat me down, took the initiative, made sure to tell me they agreed selling the house was in my best interest, both financially and emotionally, but any decision was up to me.

Anonymous, mother of four

I told her I understood that she was upset. I told her it was okay to blame me because we are on a better footing now and I can handle her disappointment. She understands and knows it was a money issue.

Anonymous, father of two

My children wanted me to sell it to them because they wanted their own children to grow up in the same environment. Thank god they both got jobs out of town. Otherwise, I have no idea how I could have sold it to one without alienating the other.

J, father of two

Selling the house was very traumatic because it brought home the fact their father had died and we would never be a whole family again. The two boys took it the hardest, perhaps because my girls had children of their own, but it wasn't easy for them either.

Anonymous, mother of five

> *Home is people. Not a place.
> If you go back there after
> the people are gone,
> then all you can see is what
> is not there anymore.*
>
> —Robin Hobb

Thirteen

Your Finances
(Wills Of The Wisp.)

Who trusts a son-in-law, really?

—Anonymous, mother of one

I intended to begin this topic with a positive, whimsical quote, similar to the one by Phyllis Diller at the end of this section.

It didn't take many interviews to discover that no matter how early parents tried to instill upon their children the value of money, of working for their allowances, of saving and not being a spendthrift, and above all, not to depend upon others (i.e. their parents) for their financial well-being, events can overtake us and even the most virtuous can be led astray.

Parents told stories of the unintended consequences of overindulgence that emotionally crippled their offspring. There was the familiar refrain that they wanted their kids to have more than they had, only to discover their ensuing sloth, substance abuse, followed by the inability to do anything for themselves, or in the more devastating instances, take care of *their* own families.

Then there was what I characterize as 'the carrot and stick scenario' and the collateral damage that followed. Like the song says, 'money can't buy you love'. What it can buy is a ruptured relationship filled with self-loathing and acrimony.

For a moment, let's take the children out of the equation and focus on us. How many of us simply don't have the adequate resources to take care of ourselves? The reason doesn't matter. We feel guilt because we can't do anything for the kids even when we want to. Then there is the associated shame that prevents us from asking for help.

Money, money, money—remember the days when all you had to worry about was how much it would take to bribe them to eat their veggies?

FYI — if you're going to cut them out of the will, don't give them power of attorney.

My sister is still controlling her forty-year-old daughter's finances, and that's not good. The daughter's always been terrible with money and my sister thinks she would go into the poorhouse, if she didn't help. I don't know if I would be any different.

B, mother of one

My son is an accountant, so he knows what I have to the last penny. He's been very good, made sure after his father died to check all our investments, deductions, and things like that. My husband took care of all the money. I never had a checkbook. I know, I know, you don't have to say anything. I'm getting much better. My son is helping. He's a blessing.

IJ, mother of one

We compartmentalized our lives, to protect them, and I think we did that with our finances as well, so it never was their concern, then or now.

Anonymous, mother of four

My finances are certainly affected by the fact there is no light at the end of the tunnel, and I have to make sure I save enough, have enough, at the end of my day, for the end of her days.

Anonymous, mother of three

My kids think I'm a doom cloud. They tease me all the time. I think it's important to have a plan and to be prepared. I think it's reality.

Anonymous, mother of two

After my husband died, my kids tried to get me to go shopping, buy the latest fashions and treat myself to some jewelry. My son even wanted me to buy a fancier car. He even wanted to take care of all my expenses. Fortunately,

I'm ok on that score, but buying all that stuff is not me. Of course, I'm appreciative, what mother wouldn't be?

Anonymous, mother of two

I decided to sign over the deed to my son, so he would have a better credit score. Unfortunately, his wife took over his finances and decided to sell my house. I was able to stop her, sell it on my own, and move into one I could afford. I should have listened to my late husband who told me not to trust her, that we hadn't seen her true side. Funny, my daughter agreed with me and, at first, liked her. We were both fooled.

Anonymous, mother of two

My kids knew everything from the time they were adolescents. Now, thank God, they do very nicely, but they still know how we're doing and thank God again, we are ok.

Anonymous, father of two

After my husband's funeral, my son-in-law discovered my medical bills and told my daughter he was going to pay for my secondary health insurance. He is a lifesaver and just a wonderful human being and the best son-in-law I could ever hope for.

M, mother of two

Said it before, we are the sandwich generation. We take care of our parents while we support our kids. The ironic thing is my generation always wanted to please our parents, so taking care of them now is just an extension of that. I don't believe my children's generation shows us the same respect and that makes helping them all the more emotionally difficult.

Anonymous, mother of six

I held an executive position, but that's gone now, and they think I'm an old lady who couldn't possibly know about finances, or could do research and learn what is necessary to make money. So, when they asked if they could recommend someone, I just said no.

Anonymous, mother of three

> *I want my children to have all the things I couldn't afford. Then I want to move in with them.*
>
> —Phyllis Diller

Fourteen

Their Finances
(Better Call Saul.)

*You know what they say...
open pocketbook, close mouth.*

—J, mother of six

I don't share J's point of view, however, having a close mouth can come in handy if you don't want to put your foot into it, and have your son accuse you of gloating because the Silicon startup he joined went belly-up.

That's just the beginning of one story I heard. Besides being greeted by the 'gloating' remark, he accused her of warning him the job wasn't going to turn out because he was a loser.

She swore to me she never called him a 'loser', but all his life she had second-guessed him, and reflecting on that, could see why he was so angry and why they had not spoken since then.

Another confessed, she called to inquire if her son's new girlfriend was after his money like the last one, only to discover the girlfriend was now his fiancé. It only got worse, because he had put the call on speaker, and the fiancé went crazy and started cursing at the mother. It took her husband to smooth things over, but she still wasn't sure she was going to be invited to the wedding.

One lady bragged she used money to gain her daughter's affection, just like her mother did with her, so, all her inquiries were welcomed because the conversation would always end by her depositing money in the daughter's account.

One parent regularly sent money to her daughter because 'she could hear the desperation in her voice'. When she let that slip out during a recent conversation with her son, he angrily accused her of favoritism, of enabling his sister to the point she depended on Mommy for her lifestyle, something he could not tolerate. They haven't spoken since.

After all my interviews, and thinking about my own relationship with my children, I believe the wise choice is to say nothing, unless they bring up the topic, and then hope you choose the right words, so even King Solomon would be envious of how wise you are.

In other words, it's none of your business if your son wants his fifteen-year-old to have an American Express Gold Card.

When I hear about her difficulties, I say, have you considered this? She comes back at me and says, "Why do you always have to tell me what to do? Can you see my problem?" She just completely misunderstands me.

Anonymous, father of two

She's a profligate. Spends more in a week than I do in a month. I don't say a word.

Anonymous, mother of two

My advice is not usually welcomed. My kids have a problem even with suggestions and even if they're sugar coated.

Anonymous, mother of four

My problem, I am worrying about their finances. I'm eighty-six, don't have much money beyond my fixed income, and neither of them are well off. And, there is nothing I can do.

Anonymous, mother of three

We don't know what to do because of our personality differences. What may be good for us may not be good for them. My mom always wanted to know about my job, how I was doing, etc. Not so my daughter, so I have learned not to ask. It hurts me.

B, mother of one

I don't like to be nosey, so I never ask, but recently my son came to me for a loan because he lost his job. Unfortunately, I just bought a car and didn't have any extra cash to give him. Now I'm feeling guilty I wasn't more on top of his situation.

LC, mother of two

He hung up on me when I innocently compared how he handled money to his sister's habits. It was only when my husband reminded me of how jealous our son became when his sister's lemonade stand outsold his, did I realize my stupidity. You can bet I never did that again.

Anonymous, mother of two

It's very disheartening that you have to leave your children their inheritance with certain parameters because they have a terrible history with their money.

Anonymous, mother of three

Like everything else, they keep us in the dark. It was only when one of my grandkids told us that his father had lost his job and needed to downsize that we knew anything was amiss. My husband was so angry he went right over and read them the riot act. They won't even talk to us, even though he gave them a considerable amount of money to tide them over.

KK, mother of one

Eric Robespierre

I told my parents everything, but my kids are different. As far as I know, they are doing fine. I learned how different they could be, from me, with my first-born, and from that experience, gave them all the space they needed. It's an interesting story. When he was young, he had a passion for collecting coins. One day, his best friend called to invite him to a movie and he said no, he was busy with his collection. I got on him, saying he could always do his coins, but having his friend's mother drive them to a movie was a special treat. He didn't see it that way. He could spend hours by himself, but I'm gregarious, need to have friends, so how could that be? I recognized my failure, and like I said, learned to give him and all my kids the space they needed and still do to this day.

J, mother of six

They all are very independent. Never ask, even the one I suspect makes just enough to get by, but in some respects, he is the happiest.

M, mother of four

Parents' responsibility is always to support them, and if it means financially until they get back on their feet, so be it. Of course, we can't enable them; tie them to our financial apron strings but that kind of issue should have been dealt with when they were teens.

Anonymous, mother of three

I have overcome financial and other difficulties by learning how to meditate. I have tried to pass that onto my son when he expresses to me how stressed he is when business is bad. I explained that meditation helps to create a more positive, settled feeling that can help weather difficult times.

Anonymous, mother of two

We never interfere with their finances and only discuss it if they ask. Again, we raised them to be independent, plus they have shown themselves to be trustworthy. Obviously, if that were not true, we might have acted differently.

Anonymous, mother of two

She goes to her father for her finances. So does her partner. However, because we are both teachers, she does come to me for work-related issues. It's less a mother/daughter thing, but more of a common sense thing. I would have a problem with it if I worked on Wall Street.

Anonymous, mother of two

Because I had several degrees, was a professional person, my daughters always came to me about questions regarding their jobs, and many times our discussions dealt with pay so naturally, they still will talk to me, maybe less since they have been married. On the really big money issues, like buying a house, or major stock investments, their husbands talk to my husband. Yes, I think it began early and that is why it continues to this day.

Anonymous, mother of two

No clue. She doesn't ask me, never talks to me either. They just moved into what I believe to be a very expensive apartment, but like I said, I have no clue what she, or her husband earn, or if they can afford it. And because of our relationship, I don't ask.

Anonymous, mother of one

He always calls his father when it has to do with business, but on more personal issues, I'm the one he talks to.

Anonymous, stepmother of one

I talk to the kids about the stock market. In fact, we use the same financial advisor. Sure, it brings us closer together.

Anonymous, father of six

I can't ask about his job because right away he becomes defensive. He thinks I'm going to get on him for not taking the job in California, which would have got him out of debt. I really only want to know if things are okay. My wife says I should just leave the subject alone.

Anonymous, father of two

Just keep paying the bills. Just keep paying for us and that's fine. How can I live with that attitude? Can't blame them. They're only twenty-one. Their brains haven't fully formed. I know mine didn't until I was twenty-five.

Anonymous, mother of two

I always thought making money was important because it showed your worth. You got paid for your services. My daughter never had a job, never had to make money. She lost a lot because of that and living on a grandmother's inheritance has spoiled her.

Anonymous, mother of two

One of my kids was looking to buy a place and my husband told me he didn't love it, but he wasn't going to say anything. He didn't want to make the same mistake his uncle did when we wanted to buy our first house. His uncle thought we didn't know the market, but really he was just afraid that because we were young, we didn't know anything.

Anonymous, mother of two

I'm fortunate that they both are doing well financially, however, I'm in a position to pick up the slack, slip them a little something as a cushion whenever I think it's appropriate.

Anonymous, father of two

After you told me about the father who picks up the slack, I have to say I do the same. Maybe not at his level because I'm on a fixed income, but yeah—I try to do it. I guess you could call it love and a responsibility to make their lives better.

Anonymous, father of one

You always hope your kids will do better than you. When they don't, you can't help thinking it was your fault. Sure, it's not rational thinking, but how you feel about your kids isn't rational, it's emotional.

Anonymous, father of four

The reality is that you are not doing your adult kids any favors by always bailing them out.

—ReShelle Barrett, certified family planner

Fifteen

Your Health
(I Could Be Younger.)

*The good news, they treat me like I'm twenty.
The bad news...
I can't babysit two toddlers and two dogs at 68.*

—Anonymous, mother of two

I am touched, to the point of tears, when I detect a slight break in my kid's voice when I reveal I have a minor health issue.

I got to thinking, what a blessing having kids that love and care about you, but on the downside, any sudden burst of emotion at my age probably poses an existential threat to my blood pressure.

I got to thinking even more, (always a mistake), and fixated on all the times you get asked about your kids and how old are they now. As your brain calculates a reply, it simultaneously mutters that must make me... Is it any wonder your pulse quickens, face heats up and your chest tightens to the point you can't breathe?

Oh, and for all you hypochondriacs, or if you're just looking for sympathy, don't email scans of a recent MRI and ask the kids if they can spot the tumor the doctors missed.

I'm trying to lighten things because it's no fun losing your health. Not only does a negative change to your health impact your life, but it also affects your children in ways not often apparent, and if not managed correctly, can have disastrous results.

While some of you are lucky enough to have a little arthritis here, a new hip there, many are facing more serious issues. Regardless of your condition, we must be open and honest with our children. If there is ever a time to treat your children as adults, it must be when we discuss the most troubling of issues.

We all want our kids to still see us, as we once were, when we lifted them on our shoulders and ran them down the block to the ice cream parlor. We can treat ourselves to the same delight if we just tell them the truth.

I don't like to talk to her about my health because it frightens her. I have to respect that.

E, mother of one

The one who lives closest always takes me to get my injections. Another, who lives a bit further, takes me for my tests. The girls understand better than the boys, maybe because I don't see them as much.

Anonymous, mother of eight

My daughter is a little bit of a hypochondriac. I think she got it from me so we're always on the phone comparing medical issues. It's my other daughter, who thinks we're both nuts... who won't take my calls unless I promise not to talk about my health. I could be lying in the street, for all she cares.

HGG, mother of three

My mother used to call me every time one of her friends died just to get me to worry about her. I vowed I would never do it to my kids.

Anonymous, mother of three

I usually don't get in between my husband and my stepson, however, because my husband seemed hesitant, I made a decision to inform my stepson of his father's medical issues. Of course, I told my husband, who didn't offer any objections because I believe, deep down; he wanted his son to know about his current situation. My stepson was grateful. Fortunately, my husband has made a full recovery.

Anonymous, stepmother of one

I go to my eldest daughter if I need to be picked up from a procedure, only because she lives closer and it is more appropriate. If need be, my other daughter is there for me as well.

M, mother of two

I just had some back issues and fortunately, she was always there for me, but it was taking care of my ex, her father, during the last year of his life that took a terrible toll on her. It wasn't until years later we talked and I realized what she was still dealing with. I could only help so much. I suggested she see a professional. She did and she's healthy again.

N, mother of two

I was a day late with my usual birthday greetings and his wife sends me literature on memory loss. My son says she was joking. I'm not looking forward to this Thanksgiving. I can tell you that.

Anonymous, mother of one

My eldest, she lives the closest, but she ignores me. (Laughs). She's a lot like me. (Laughs again.) Doesn't come to visit but she was there for me when I was sick. And on holidays, always here, or I go to her place.

Anonymous, mother of three

*They never ask, so I assume they
don't care. Sure it bothers me.*

Anonymous, mother of three

*I know you're probably talking about physical
health, but I'm reminded of what someone said.
'Our generation has too much guilt, this one,
not enough.' Perhaps that explains some of the
problems we have with our adult children.*

Anonymous, father of six

*Of course, I would rather be younger and healthier,
but some good things evolve over time, like the
fact one of my daughters no longer blames me
for everything that went wrong in her life.*

Anonymous, mother of three

*I don't think they are taking advantage of me. They
look at me and still see the mother, who was young,
fit and could handle anything. I just have to let them
know when I get tired, when I can't handle things.*

Anonymous, mother of two

Knock on wood I'm okay, and so is my husband. It's been over twenty years of sobriety for us, so I'm always making sure we all have our physicals, checking to be sure no damage has been done. It's a subject that is always on everyone's mind but not talked about.

Anonymous, mother of two

*After my husband's funeral, my son-in-law discovered my medical bills and told my daughter he was going to pay for my secondary health insurance.

M, mother of two

> *Always be nice to your children because they are the ones who will choose your rest home.*
>
> —Phyllis Diller

---

* I know this is a repeat, but it's just as fitting here and a reminder of how caring and loving family can be.

Sixteen

Their Health
(They Should Live And Be Well.)

My only hope is to live long enough to see him get help.

—Anonymous, mother of three

As parents, our worst fear is that we will outlive our children. This angst can morph into patterns of self-destructive behavior that threaten to alienate our adult children. One of my kids flies frequently for business, and in the beginning, I'd check weather reports and keep an eye out for breaking news fearing an airline catastrophe. I don't think he sensed my anxiety, but after a while, I recognized my problem and now, beyond the normal messages that sincerely reflect my wishes for a safe and successful trip, I don't give it a second thought.

When one of our children suffers an illness, our ability to stay calm and simply be there to show our love and support can be sorely tested. The axiom, 'We are as happy as our saddest child,' is often quoted in these pages. The word 'healthiest' can be substituted for 'saddest' with the same maddening impact.

What my parent interviews have taught me is, no matter how old our progenies, when they become ill, we can easily revert back to treating them like little children. Sometimes they take comfort in this, but many have outgrown that relationship and react poorly to this approach.

In times of stress, first and foremost, we must be sensitive to *their* needs, and never let our fears get in the way of their speedy recovery.

As one mother so eloquently stated, "Put on your brave face and don't f'ing take it off until you get home, have a stiff drink and then a good cry!"

One last thought. If you want them to quit smoking, at least you could have enclosed a package of Nicorettes along with the selfies of you lighting an entire row of church candles.

We had no idea she was on drugs. She was a straight arrow. We're still reeling from it, wished we could have stopped it.

Anonymous, mother of three

*My daughter is a bit of a hypochondriac. I think she got it from me, so we're always on the phone comparing medical issues. It's my other daughter, who thinks we're both nuts. Who won't take my calls,

---

* *Quote works here as well as in previous chapter.*

unless I promise not to talk about my health problems. I could be laying in the street, for all she cares.

HGG, mother of three

I always listen, then, I try to illicit some sort of action plan. I have to be very careful because when they talk about their health, I immediately become very anxious and I have to hide my anxiety, or it just compounds the problem.

K, mother of two

This is how I handle it. I throw it back and try to get their take on things—you know, ask them what they think. Unfortunately, they know my game and they get angry, tell me they wouldn't be calling if they knew the answers. Then it becomes tricky, because I have to be careful I don't criticize, make them feel defensive. Of course, it all depends on how serious, the health issue is. So far, thank God, only minor problems with them or their kids.

L, mother of three

He was diagnosed with Type 1 diabetes when he was an infant and we almost lost him a couple of times. He did a few foolish things when he was a teenager, but basically he's been responsible and is in good health. Don't kid yourself, no matter how old they are, you still worry about them—maybe not worry, worry. Just now and then.

Anonymous, father of two

Eric Robespierre

He's over forty but still suffers from headaches and he will frequently come over and I'll rub his head, just like I did when he was a child. No, his wife doesn't know.

Anonymous, mother of two

Sometimes my advice is taken, sometimes it's not, but they all know I'm not a control freak, a worrywart; so my concerns are genuine, and by and large, I think they take them to heart.

S, mother of four

My son is a bit of a hypochondriac and coincidently, my daughter is a physician, so he's always calling her and she's setting him straight. I get this from her or at least what she wants to share that doesn't infringe on his privacy.

Anonymous, mother of two

My stepson has diabetes and we had to watch him during childhood and into adolescents. Now that he's an adult, he manages well with the pump and we are no longer anxious about his heath. However, it's always in the back of our minds, and we are just grateful he always took his medical condition seriously and continues to act responsibly.

Anonymous, stepmother of one

Even though they are adults, you still worry about them, especially if they have an ongoing medical issue like diabetes. We had to watch him when he was young and those memories are still very strong, especially when he made some youthful mistakes. Thankfully, now that he has the pump keeping him stabilized, we aren't as anxious.

Anonymous, stepmother of one

When I noticed he had a problem I asked if he thought it would be a good idea to put him into rehab? He looked at me strangely and the next day he checked himself into the hospital. I'm lucky he lives nearby, I can see for myself how he's living and that I can talk to him without having him get defensive and shutting me out.

Anonymous, mother of two

I have spoken in general terms about his smoking, and he knows not to smoke, but I don't harp on it. He's an adult.

S, mother of two

I found what worked was to discuss with him ways to change, ways he thinks he wants his life to be. Says his therapist tells him the same thing.

Anonymous, mother of two

Eric Robespierre

The hardest thing to do is respect her boundaries when it comes to her weight, especially when right in front of me, she is stuffing her face with all those snacks.

Anonymous, father of two

Anything can set him off. It's not so much what I said, but how he reacts to the outside world and it's all about self-esteem. Believe me, he's handsome, charismatic, yet totally without confidence and I'm sure that's what led to his addiction. I just have to continue to praise him and hope for the best.

Anonymous, mother of three

Two fathers. One was an addict, the other... not. Two kids with the addict, both of them had issues. The other... not. Biological?

Anonymous, mother of two

Don't think I haven't thought about running in place wearing a tracksuit outside his window. Maybe, if I were thirty years younger, I'd do it.

Anonymous, mother of one

I want to say it's never too late. Never burn bridges, no matter how uncommunicative, how unwilling your children are to call, return calls. Don't shut down and end all contact. I followed that advice, and after not hearing from my son in quite a while, called, without anger, recriminations, only holiday cheer and love. Unexpectedly, he confessed how much trouble he was having with his own son, and then, for the first time, told me about his own physical problems. He thanked me for calling, showing interest and told me he loved me.

L, mother of two

Because his father would pass him on the street and not even say hello, I had to make up for it with unconditional love. Is that why he won't engage? The psychologist just gave me that diagnosis, didn't say my behavior was the cause. Bottom line, we don't communicate.

Anonymous, mother of one

I'm always looking for ways to suggest how he can change, see a life without drugs. He tells me that's what his therapist tells him. At least he didn't hang up the phone.

Anonymous, mother of one

After losing one daughter to drugs and alcohol, it's natural you worry even more about the two that are still alive.

Anonymous, mother of three

Doesn't matter how old they are, you still remember their problems and give them a pass, provide financial support. I know it's wrong, his sister tells me so every time we talk.

Anonymous, mother of two

Both kids are in good health, except they're overweight and that bothers me. Unfortunately, I slipped a few times with my daughter, but I've learned to keep my mouth shut. My father had a saying. 'If you have to tell somebody something twice, then give it up. Never say it again because they will never listen'.

Anonymous, mother of two

She can't sleep and she appreciates my help, my input, that sometimes puts things in perspective and helps her relax so she can get a good night's sleep.

Anonymous, mother of one

Sobriety has always been a genetic problem and my husband and I worry about our kids, but we are careful not to put them on the defensive; just watch and see how they are doing.

Anonymous, mother of two

I had no idea she was doing drugs. My husband and I were ignorant of the signs, or shall I say the lack of them. She looked fine, did great in school...

Anonymous, mother of two

When they have a history of addiction, you're always living like they are, from day to day. The real travesty is that once they reach eighteen, you cannot take control of their lives without their consent. It really leaves you powerless. We are talking fifty years. It takes a toll. Somehow you have to cope.

Anonymous, mother of three

He has a lot of problems being a grown-up and dealing with people. I don't want to go into the psychological reasons.

Anonymous, mother of two

I'm eighty-six and I worry about my daughter's health when she holds up pro-abortion signs outside abortion clinics because I know her life has been threatened.

Anonymous, mother of three

Eric Robespierre

She was drinking and drugging, getting involved with the police and I asked her to leave. Of course it haunts me, twenty years later, especially since she's still doing it.

Anonymous, mother of three

You have to be aware of their changes. Then, when they get into trouble, drugs, alcohol, I tell them to believe in God. For my eldest, that, and that he wanted to save his marriage, and start a new career, going to church helped him. My daughter, has been much harder because starting when she was young, she suffered from depression, was into drugs. She became dependent on men for her happiness and when they left, it was bad. Thank God she's cleaned up her act after giving birth. She has a job, lives with her daughter in a halfway house and goes to church. My other boy, he doesn't go to church, doesn't do drugs. I see him drunk sometimes and he's got a few exes, live-ins, a whole bunch of kids I take care of. Always have to love them and give them support, try to keep the family together. I was in an orphanage, separated from my brothers and sisters so maybe it's more important for me.

Anonymous, mother of three

We Gave Them Life, Now They're Trying To Take Ours

> *The man who asks a question*
> *is a fool for a minute,*
> *the man who does not ask is a fool for life.*
>
> —Confucius

Seventeen

Holidays
(You In The Spirit?)

*I hate 'em. They're all over the place.
Not like when I was growing up and
everyone lived within five blocks of each other.*

—Anonymous, mother of six

After listening to my interviewees, I discovered there were three camps they put themselves in. My anonymous mother of six is in the group that can't cope with the impossible logistics of getting the family under one roof for the holidays. As J, a mother of five, and another proud member, so graphically painted her predicament: "It's worse than corralling a group of wild horses after they've jumped the fence and headed into the wild."

The second group had a darker take, and no one expressed that more candidly than my anonymous mother of three when rhetorically she spat: "Tell me—why would anyone bring ribs when she knows we're vegetarians? Because she hates me!"

I belong to the third group, 'the extended family'. This, of course, is the gentle euphemism for those of us who are a product of divorce. For our members, holidays can mean interacting with your ex, or multiple exes. Then there are the exes of the adult children. Let's not forget *their* extended family. Multiple half-brothers and sisters, the various sets of in-laws, etc., etc., etc., ... all of whom show up, or don't. Causing even more discord.

Extended families also bring with them a whole host of religious and non- religious beliefs, made more complex and difficult to comprehend, or appreciate, because of language and cultural barriers.

Surprises are to be avoided. Open and total communication must be achieved before your son in-laws, in-laws, come directly from the boat with a tethered lamb ready to be slaughtered. That goes for anything else that might cause Customs, The World Health Organization, or The Centers for Disease Control to come knocking at your door.

Let's not forget Interpol. They do not look kindly to your newest relative, who also happens to be a grave robber (a lucrative and not frowned-upon occupation in some countries), bringing you a house-warming gift freshly unearthed from the tomb of Queen Nefertiti.

I guarantee none of these visitors are bringing frankincense and myrrh, also a no-no if there are atheists and agnostics in the family.

Finally, please remember, the holidays are not the time to serve divorce papers, childhood support bills, or restraining orders.

I cut the umbilical cord. I'm happy when I see them. I love my kids and I want to be around them. I go up, or they come down for the holidays. But I have a wonderful life.

J, mother of six

You would think when she had a child of her own, my daughter would invite us for the holidays, but she's still carrying grudges. Oh, nothing against my husband. She's always been his favorite. It's me. I'm overbearing and she doesn't want me to be a bad influence on her children. My god, the child was just born.

Anonymous, mother of two

When my son suggested I mend fences and invite his father to Christmas dinner, I said ok. I ate crow, which was what I wanted to serve the SOB, but I didn't. (Laugher)

Anonymous, mother of one

My new daughter in-law knows I like to have Christmas at my house, so my two daughters and their husbands can come from out of town and stay over, but she insists on their house, ten miles from mine. We would have to rent another car, plus it's tiny, and every one would have to eat buffet-style, in two rooms. My husband won't let me say anything and my two daughters just won't come.

SD, mother of three

Staying with my son is like being at a B&B. Staying with my daughter, always knew something was going on, but I couldn't put my finger on it, always couldn't wait to leave.

Anonymous, mother of two

One of my daughter's celebrates some holidays in New York. Another wants us to come to her place, in a part of New Jersey, which is a distance from my son who lives nearer to me. We are all over the place, but we try to celebrate at least one holiday all together, so the cousins can get to see each other, but it's very difficult. No, there is no animosity and I never complain.

Anonymous, mother of three

My parents would be turning over in their graves if they knew what was going on with my kids, but I have to deal with reality. We're not all living in the same neighborhood anymore. And I'm not talking about the ones who live out of state. I'm talking about the ones who live twenty miles this way and fifteen miles that way. I have to let it go. They have their own lives and sure, I suffer, the cousins suffer, because none of us get to see each other. But you cannot risk alienating them by making a big deal out of it.

Anonymous, mother of three

Talk about crazy. My sister invited the person who officiated at her daughter's first wedding to last year's Thanksgiving.

S, mother of two

Holidays are difficult to keep track of, so I keep a book. I write where I go, and when, so the next year I know where I'm supposed to be.

P, mother of two

When they were young, I loved to celebrate the holidays at our home. Now, I need to accommodate their needs and we manage the traffic. Never say anything, just make it a point to leave two hours earlier. We do curse a lot when we're on the parkway. (Laughing)

Anonymous, mother of three

For one of my sons, since my divorce, he misses the family unit. That's why, whenever there is a family function, he's ready to go. Holidays, that is the most important time for him to see me. My other two children—one, not so much, the other she couldn't care less. Sure it hurts. What mother wouldn't want all her children to be with her for the holidays, family functions like birthdays, graduations, etc.?

Anonymous, mother of three

Despite the fact that I cannot say boo to her without being called out for being too critical, when it comes to Thanksgiving, when I have at least thirty people coming over, she happily takes over and does everything for me—from the cooking to the cleaning up. She relieves me of all the stress. Crazy, huh? (Pause) Don't I wish every day was Thanksgiving...

Anonymous, mother of one

When last Thanksgiving came I was hoping he would email me, or something. I don't even know his street address. (Crying.) He didn't.

Anonymous, mother of one

I never put pressure on my kids to come see me for the holidays, or to live near me. Sure, I regret that they don't, but I don't regret my actions. I wanted them to be independent. They have their own busy lives. I go to see them. Of course, as I get older and transportation becomes more difficult, it bothers me more.

Anonymous, mother of three

I don't see my son much during the holidays because his wife tries to keep him all to herself. When they come around, I remember when he was a teen he asked if his biological parents were rich. I said no. I asked why he would ask? He said now, that we are coming into the holidays and because they didn't take care of me all those years, I thought I could ask them to pay for my college tuition.

Anonymous, mother of two

When we try to get my son to come to an event, he calls it a command performance.

Anonymous, father of six

On my birthday, the one still at home will show some interest, but the one at school just sends a text with 'love yah'. Their brains aren't fully formed, so I can't blame them.

Anonymous, mother of two

Because of our split, this is the roughest time. Traditions like having Christmas one place, Thanksgiving another, is now totally screwed up. I have to leave the state, so I don't become an object of pity. All you can do is keep your conscience clear. To do that, you have to be strong. If not, you are just going to get hurt.

Anonymous, father of two

*Tell me why would anyone bring ribs when she knows we are vegetarians? Because she hates me!

Anonymous, mother of two

---

*   I just had to repeat this one!

*Get into the spirit of the season.
This is a time of giving,
forgiving, and fresh starts.
Turn Scrooge's emotional
lessons about holidays
past, present, and yet to come
into New Year's resolutions
about letting go of anger and
treasuring all you have –
despite all you have lost.*

—Robert E. Emery PhD

Eighteen

Vacations
(Part 1. Togetherness.)

If you're taking a teen make sure nothing in your wardrobe is as old as the kid.

—Anonymous grandmother of four

My interviews have resulted in these findings. If history points to a relatively well-functioning family, where trips to restaurants, malls and amusement parks didn't result in the police calling Family Services, traveling with adult children will be just as pleasant with memories to last a lifetime. If, on the other hand, those excursions were even more catastrophic than those in the Griswold *Family Vacation* movies—don't even think about it!

There are all sorts of family vacations, each bringing their own set of possible calamities. There is the cruise where so many activities separate families until everyone sits down at the co-mingling dinner table to socialize. Either your progenies will make you beam with pride retelling how you guys drove twenty miles every morning to take them to soccer practice, or, seeing the opportunity to make the mid-Western Church folks at the other end gag on their food, confess how when they were five, you had them pick fruit from sun-up until their tiny, bleeding, fingers couldn't hold the oranges in their hands a second longer.

Then there is the trip back to the 'old country'. Your unhappy child now can point to the origins of your inability to 'understand them' as they gleefully mocked those provincial souls who feverishly crossed themselves when confronted with pasty faced, black lipped grandchildren, dressed as Goths.

Be especially wary of trips requiring extra life and accident insurance. Not saying that had anything to do with Phil's kids inheriting five million, but strange they came back from the kayaking misadventure and dear ole dad has yet to be found.

Then there is the laying by the pool having nothing to do all day but drink oneself into a stupor. Talk about loose lips that sink ships. You're going to go down faster than you can say Titanic after a dozen piña coladas and suddenly you're the one to blame for your daughter's low self-esteem. "Who the fuck wants to be called 'Pookiekins' all their fucking life!" Even now, you can't remember if it was the other rummies at the pool who clapped, or was it her idea to dive naked into the pool, sending the barman into the hotel for the defibrillator.

Lest we forget the ' X Family Reunion' when you spot your eldest swapping spit with a first cousin, or sharing recipes for producing illegal substances that make Walter White look like an amateur.

Look, if you can't face the possibility of being in the next Griswold movie, just pick the one exotic destination requiring the most painful vaccinations... you know how much they hate needles.

I keep thinking I shouldn't have let my youngest go off after college because now she is so busy, the only time I see her and her family, is during vacations, or in the case coming up, a wedding in France. It's not really a time for fun and games when you haven't seen them in so long and all you want to do is catch up and that may mean some serious discussions.

Anonymous, mother of three

Lots of tension, even if you are on vacation, and if you pay attention, you will see it, and I pay attention to everything. Not fun when you see your kid's marriage falling apart.

Anonymous, mother of two

She wanted me to go on vacation with her and her boys. She hates to drive. Also knows I'm not so crazy about it so she's going to hire a car. I can imagine, me without a car, and she becomes abusive. I'm stranded. Not going until we have a sit-down and I find out where she is. Not putting myself in that position, no way, no how.

Anonymous, mother of two

She told me I was not permitted to go with them and their kids. If I ignored her, she wouldn't go. The reason for the vacation was so the grandkids could get together because they don't see each other too often. So, I didn't go. Sometime later, we got together and she showed me a picture of all the kids. I thought that was mean.

Anonymous, mother of two

It occurred to me that I'm in good shape, have energy, have the resources, so when I heard about this intergenerational tour, I thought, if I don't start taking them now, creating memories, when will I? So, the most logical approach would be to start with my eldest and every year, work my way down to the youngest of the four.

B, mother of two

I don't get along with my daughter-in-law, but when I suggested I take her youngest, who is twelve, on a trip my granddaughter hesitated because she really is tied to her mother's apron strings. To my surprise, her mother said—you know your grandmother isn't getting any younger and she, will not be available forever.

Anonymous, mother of three

I just returned from taking my fourteen-year-old to Italy. It was quite an experience. Several times she said she needed quiet time and I respected her need to rest, relax, read or contact her friends on social media. Very grown-up.

B, mother of two

It's funny, my daughter and I are both afraid of confrontation and maybe that's what makes us great traveling companions. Or, it just could be that from childhood to adulthood we both like the same things, art, architecture, different climates, and cultures.

Anonymous, mother of two

My granddaughter scolded me for saying I tell people what to do. No, I explained, I just tell people they shouldn't do things if I think they are wrong. Case in point. Our gondolier. He was making a personal call, and was so loud it was distracting to the point we couldn't enjoy the scenery. It distracted him from doing his job, which was to safely guide us along the canals. I told him to stop and he did. I believe she, like many her age, gets a little intimidated in public. Hopefully, my example will teach her to speak up now.

B, mother of two

Naturally, there are little spats, shouts, temper flare-ups when you're on top of each other, and don't have the privacy you're accustomed to, especially, when you're a teen and privacy is so important. She did tell me, I have something to tell you—you're awesome. Out of all the grandmothers on the cruise you were the one who was unforgettable. Kids loved you the best because you were the coolest. I'm seventy-seven. Was that great or what?

Anonymous, mother of three

Never again! Too much anxiety! Lots of tension between them because when they're with me and my husband she wants him to show her attention, show he cares for her and the children but that's not the way he is in private.

Anonymous, mother of one

> *In America, there are two classes of travel: first-class and with children*
>
> —Robert Benchley

Nineteen

Vacations
(Part 2. Home Alone?)

I'm not saying frat house life informed my opinion of my thirty-five year -old son and his wife, but...

—M, father of one

Let me tell you, this topic really got my parents going. For instance...

"I'm holding my breath whenever my son and his two crazies come over for the holidays. Believe me... they'd destroy anything not nailed down. Think I'd let 'em in here while my wife and I are away?"

And this one...

"There wasn't any reason not to trust him—he had never gotten into trouble—we knew his friends. So, we went on our two-week Caribbean vacation. When we got home, the place was in shambles! Drawers were opened, contents thrown on the floor; beds were unmade; liquor and beer bottles all over—cigarette burns on the couch. I'm not saying he would do that again. He's got a wife, good job, but things like that make it hard to trust someone, even twenty-five years later."

On the flip side, I had one mother tell me she looked forward to going away so the grandkids could have their own room, swim in the pool anytime they wanted, and have a vacation all their own without grandpa and grandma hovering over them.

Another had a more devious motive. She wanted her daughter and her family to leave the city and move back into the neighborhood where she grew up. My interviewee even had dreams of giving the house to her, but she knew how resistant the daughter was to any notion of living outside of Brooklyn. Her plan was simple. She began going on vacations during the summer, when she knew her grandchild would want to go swimming in the pool and generally take advantage of all the suburbs had to offer. So far it hasn't worked, but she has booked vacations for the next three summers and is hoping for the best.

If you're going to hide the 'welcome mat', make sure you put it where you know the kids won't find it—like the dishwasher. Remember, too, bullet proofing the house doesn't mean turning off all the utilities. And for all you fans of 'Post-It Notes'… a smiley face emoji doesn't soften messages like: 'Open liquor cabinet, cops will respond, no bail money!

I wish they would visit, and if I could afford it, I would build a pool, but they're too busy to take time off from work to come cross-country. I have to go to them.

Anonymous, mother of three

I remembered what I did to my parent's home when they went away, and I sure as hell wasn't going to repeat their mistake with my kid, then, or now. I've seen what their kids do to their place.

Anonymous, mother of one

I had to downsize because of my age but I do miss the fact I just don't have the room anymore so they could come and spend the night, let alone play in the backyard.

Anonymous, mother of one

He accused me of being a 'mean' grandfather because I lock the playroom when I go away. He knows how expensive my trains are, and he also knows that even when I'm there, I only let them take the controls, or touch the trains under my supervision. He also knows they break everything they touch.

Anonymous, father of one

I'm not saying my daughter-in-law is the one who went through my drawers, but she was certainly responsible for making damn sure my granddaughter didn't. I'm thinking of putting a Nanny Cam into the bedroom.

Anonymous, mother of one

*In the past, I had no trouble going away and having my
son and his family stay, for as long as they wanted—
that is until my divorce lawyer asked if I could trust
them not to rummage around and look for anything that
my wife could use against me in court. I had no idea
what he meant, but it made me so uneasy. I decided
to postpone any trip until my divorce is finalized.*

Anonymous, father of one

> *If you are a parent,
> open doors to unknown
> directions to the child
> so he can explore.
> Don't make him afraid of the unknown,
> give him support.*
>
> —Osho

Twenty

Vacations
(Part 3. Three Day Old Fish, etc...)

*As soon as they stop calling me Grandpa
and refer to me as 'him'
I know it's time to go.*

—Anonymous, father of one

I don't usually repeat stories other parents tell me, saving them for when they read them in this book, however, when the parent I'm quoting above thought he had it rough, I relayed the experience of the visiting mom who nearly tumbled out of bed when the room reverberated with the roar of her twin grandsons' drum duos.

One parent told me; with the help of Xanax, she no longer antagonizes her daughter-in-law, and thus made peace with her son, by no longer scrubbing all the bathtubs in the house. Although, she continues to secretly sanitize the one in the guest room.

Want to know what I've learned? Don't feign illness or injury so you can stay an extra week. If it is an injury, remember, you don't actually have to break anything to make it look real. And last, but certainly not least, remember you're a guest in your child's house, not visiting a hotel or spa. So, no requests like European Breakfast, Apricot Cleansings or Same-day Dry Cleaning.

My ex has poisoned the well, and even though I'm welcomed to stay, there is a chill in the air that makes me very uncomfortable. Add to that, all those photos of her on the refrigerator and I just want to get out of there. Too bad, before the breakup I just loved visiting with them, making them their favorite pasta dishes.

Father, another of four

I usually go up for three days and it's very stressful because I have to fit everything into that time frame; birthdays, school functions, sports, entertainment events, etc., etc., etc. The three kids are of different ages, so I can't bunch them up. I always end up spending all my time with the grandkids, and never have enough serious time for my own son and his wife. And you're right; I can't stay longer than the three days… just like fish….

Anonymous, mother of three

The key to staying at their place is to never upset their routine, or get in the way of the wife, or the dog.

Anonymous, mother of three

I'm always respectful of their space when I stay with them. It's a second sense, have that instinct to go out onto the porch, or take a short walk when I think I may be in the way.

Anonymous, mother of two

I am always aware of my stepdaughter's needs and make sure I don't overstep my bounds and we never have a problem.

Anonymous, stepmother of one

If they lived closer I could drop by for an hour, but when they are so far away I have to stay for two to three days and things become forced. You need to cover a lot of ground, and it can seem like a non-stop question-and-answer session, and that's no fun. No time for small talk, or just relaxing with them, or the grandchildren. I don't know if it's them or me, but after two days, I want to leave.

Anonymous, mother of three

We had the best of all worlds until age caught up with my husband and me and now we're trapped. During the year, we travel to St Louis and stay for a week. In the summer we go and stay with them in Boca for maybe ten days. We don't mind that my daughter and her husband might take a short trip, and leave us to babysit, but like I said, as we got older we just can't keep up with teens anymore. We're trying to figure out how to get our message across. Oh, sure, we thought they'd see it, but I guess they always want us to stay young.

P&R, parents of one

It's the pictures of my ex that make it uncomfortable. They are all over. On the fridge, in the living room—see what I mean? Thank goodness they removed the ones from the guest room. What can I say? It's their house.

Anonymous, father of one

> *Uselessness, she thought, was the permanent condition of parenthood.*
>
> —Lisa Unger, *Fragile*

Twenty-One

In-laws
(Don't Go There!)

*When he came to me with in-law problems
I knew the two of us watching
Father Knows Best back in the day was the right move.*

—Anonymous, father of one

My heart sank when I heard that. I watched *Dirty Harry* movies with my kids. Could I expect my progenies to come and confide they needed help in buying a .44 Magnum to solve their In-law problems?

What about fathers who feasted on *Alien, Damian* or *The* Exorcist with their impressionable youngins? It's a dark road from which there is no coming back if you agree with your daughter that her father-in-law is the Antichrist.

If you fear your daughter-in-law wants to separate you from your son, don't feign illness, or even worse have your priest or rabbi call from your 'death bed.

On the subject of fibbing, you have to have a death wish if you claim you got food poisoning from your daughter-in-law's cooking.

If you want peace to reign in providence, for the multilingual *ferme la bouche* and for the rest of us—just zip it.

And if you don't want to follow my advice… do you feel lucky? Well, do ya, punk?

My son-law has a mother who thinks she's his sister. How sick is that? I was waiting for her to do the same to my daughter, but she never did. Not that I would say anything. I learned to shut up.

Anonymous, mother of two

He got married and that's when the trouble started.

Anonymous, mother of three

They moved there because they didn't want any family dropping in all the time. I had mixed feelings. I need my space, so I respected that, but still they were far away.

Anonymous, mother of one

She hated me from day minus one. She's very jealous, very possessive. I think she resents me because she never had a relationship with her mother and she is envious of my relationship with my son. I say nothing. My son says nothing.

Anonymous, mother of two

We are fairly private with each other. I would never say that one son-in-law is a pain in the ass.

Anonymous, mother of three

Her father-in-law is Sephardic. Very family oriented, clannish, secretive. I like to joke, say my daughter married into a Jewish mob. Don't get me wrong, they're very nice to me, but I know I'm an outsider.

Anonymous, mother of one

His mother was very strange. Ran hot and cold. Would come in and maybe say hello or not. Would leave, never say anything. Better when she had more to drink. I kept my mouth shut but couldn't wait to get the hell out of there.

Anonymous, mother of two

There is a thin veneer covering their behavior. Look around the large, expensive house and these gorgeous children—everybody is well dressed, plenty of money — everybody is well nourished, perfectly coiffed, but the men never stay monogamous. The wife doesn't care. Give me lots of diamonds, maids, leave me alone. Do whatever you want. I know this kills my daughter.

Anonymous, mother of one

My son converted because his in-laws said they would disown their daughter if he didn't convert to Catholicism. I blame myself because I didn't say no, object more strongly, but we were never that religious. Very confusing.

Anonymous, mother of two

With my son it's not so much walking on eggshells. I just have to be careful what I say or ask because everything gets back to my daughter-in-law. She is a good person, but she can be mean. She can misunderstand things. I only can talk to my son in generalities. I can't talk deeply on the phone because she's always listening in, and it's totally impossible when I'm over there. She's very suspicious, a little paranoid. You can say I'm afraid to get him alone, don't know what will get back to her.

N, mother of two

Her father-in-law, the multi-millionaire, gives my grandson a bar mitzvah in Israel. He gives my granddaughter a bat mitzvah in Philly. You figure it out. I say nothing.

Anonymous, mother of one

She doesn't like anyone who belongs to him. I wonder if it's a woman-to-woman thing because I never hear fathers having this kind of problem with their daughters-in-law.

Anonymous, mother of five

My second husband's mother was in a wheelchair, and when I asked one of the sisters, she said it was menopause. I said, are you kidding? If that was the case you couldn't walk down the streets of New York without getting run over. My step kids never knew I said that because they were very close to her and would have given me grief.

S, mother of one, stepmother of three

She keeps him from his friends, his sister and me. I know it has been especially harmful to my daughter, but I cannot say anything to him, or else it will get back to her.

N, mother of two

I love my daughter-in-laws parents, but I hate my daughter-in-law. Go figure?

Anonymous, mother of one

They say when you marry your spouse, you don't marry their family. Boy what a load of crap. From the start, I had problems with his mother who always thought I wasn't good enough for her son. Now, I'm having problems with my son's mother-in-law, who thinks the same thing. My husband says it's me that's seeing problems when there aren't any. He only said it once. He knows what's good for him.

Anonymous, mother of one

You know, you don't want to rock the boat, but then you never get anything resolved. I detected a bit of anti-Semitism when one of my in-laws said something about their neighbor. But I never said anything about it to my son, and, as a consequence, I don't know if I was reading something into it that wasn't there. If it was, is that one of the reasons they made him convert? Made his wife give me the silent treatment, made him estranged from me? See what I mean about not confronting your kids? Could it have resulted in anything worse than what it is now? I don't know, but that's who I am.

Anonymous, mother of one

> *The natural state of the sentient adult is qualified unhappiness.*
>
> —F. Scott Fitzgerald, *The Crack Up*

Twenty-Two

Social Media
(Kumbaya!)

I'm the Texting Queen. Who would have thought?

—S, mother of two

Yep. Who would have thought? You with no typing abilities and fingers too large for those small keys, but when your eight-year-old granddaughter couldn't wait to text you what she wore to school, or your son, his running commentary during *Game of Thrones*—you found some skills quick enough, didn't you?

As you will see, social media cannot cure all ills, but even in the worst case, it does provide parents with another way to reach out and open communication with their kids in a form that is easily accessible to everyone.

I just wish advertisers, depicting that kumbaya moment when families get the phone plan, making it possible to talk and text to their hearts content would include grandma and grandpa in plan. Sure, we may have a touch of arthritis, but we can jump up and down with the best of them.

Eric Robespierre

Nothing replaces the human voice, but you must go with the flow and if that means texting, you do it. I do stop with Facebook because I'm a very private person, and thank God, so are my kids.

B, father of two

I have a solution for all that desire you have to meddle in their lives, like following them on social media—get a life.

J, mother of six

They Facetime me and we use the WhatsApp. Send photos back and forth to my kids, grandkids. It really connects like never before.

J, mother of two

The construct that would make her the most comfortable is e-mail.

B, mother of two

No tones available. Just texting. I'll go with it.

B, mother of two

Their mother is very jealous of me, but now that they have their own phones, my granddaughters and I—we have started this little texting thing.

Anonymous, mother of two

I really can't get through a conversation without a certain friend picking up her iPhone for a call, text or Facetime from one of her children. I find it annoying because her kids are so dependent, and obviously, my friend is too. Social media can be just too much of an enabler for parents who engage in that kind of smothering relationship with their children. It is also rude on her part and my feelings don't come into the equation. Obviously, I avoid being around her if possible.

Anonymous, mother of two

I find out too much about them from seeing what they post online. I'm a very private person, so I don't approve. My wife is more vocal and tells my daughter how she feels. Doesn't go down well.

Anonymous, father of two

I have a running conversation with my daughters via texting, but they're so fast, I'm always falling behind. It's fun and I have to admit, brings us all closer together.

Anonymous, mother of two

I used to take pictures of me and other people, in social situations, but I had to take any off my Facebook account that had women in them because my soon to be divorced wife told my kids those were the women I was fooling around with. I'm tired of being misinterpreted.

Anonymous, father of two

We text. Got me out of the dark ages and into a modern relationship with my daughter.

H, mother of two

No matter how many problems we have with our kids, social media keeps us in close contact with the grandkids. We exchange text messages and they send photos of the snow up north when we are in Florida. Lucky. That's what we are.

Anonymous, father of six

She never told me, and if it weren't for Facebook, I wouldn't have known about her car accident. She wasn't badly hurt, but it did total her car. No, I didn't confront her about it. That wouldn't have changed her attitude toward sharing, probably would have made her un-friend me, or whatever they do to keep me from seeing her page.

Anonymous, mother of three

I would never post anything on social media that would affect our relationship in a negative way. In conversations, if I did that, I would immediately apologize, but on social media there is no taking it back, plus the world can see it.

B, mother of two

I have a disagreement with my daughter because I don't appreciate being posted online. I don't want everyone to know what I'm doing. Don't want to share my life with everyone. She likes to keep up-to-day with her high school friends. I understand that, however, we all have to be very cautious, too much going on, too scary today. She says she's very careful, so I have to trust her. One last thing, I told her if she posts my death on Facebook I'll haunt you!. No, no problem with my son. He feels the same way about Facebook as I do.

Anonymous, mother of two

We text, we are on Facebook, and they send photos. At the end of the year, they take all those photos and make books out of them and give them to us as Xmas presents.

C, mother of three

I'm afraid to go on Facebook because I don't know what she writes about me, or her family. I get the occasional birthday card, so that encourages me to believe some lines of positive communication are still open. Nevertheless, I don't trust her to write anything positive about us.

Anonymous, mother of two

We Facetime, then, joined Instagram to see pictures of the babies. It's wonderful, especially since they live so far away.

Anonymous, mother of two

I'll tell you the truth, I like to hear their voices, but if you don't text, you're out of luck. Texting is a good thing, though. They answer right away, more immediate contact. I think they're sitting there with their phone. In my case, no Facetime because they're always busy and you have to make an appointment.

Anonymous, mother of three

I'm sorry; I want to hear their voices. How else will I get a real feel for their emotions — emojis?

The author, father of two

> *In this age of instant communication, emoticons are replacing words, body language replacing language and visuals replacing text.*
>
> —Haresh Sippy

Twenty-Three

Politics
(The Elephant In The Room.)

*Half my family voted for Donald Trump
and half for Hillary Clinton–
now the hatred between us
has reached a fever pitch.*

—Skylar Baker-Jordan

My views on politics was formed by H. L. Mencken's cynical belief that if a politician found he had cannibals among his constituents, he would promise them missionaries for dinner. Therefore, it never crossed my mind to add a chapter on the subject, until the 2016 campaign morphed into Mr. Trump's presidency and my interviewees made it the first thing they talked about.

I was shocked to see that the acrimony, so evident in public discourse, had insidious ramifications within the family unit, sowing so much discord, that in some cases, parents were no longer talking to their children. The above quote from Skylar Baker-Jordan is indicative of this cacophony.

Another group of interviewees decided to put the love for their children above all else, and either never brought the subject up, or when it did, bit their tongue and said nothing that would in any way antagonize their kids

I want to repeat, I'm not writing this book to pass judgment, or tell you what you should do. I'm here to make sure you know you are not alone, and these problems, in all their manifestations, are not yours alone. They are issues that face us all.

You have to make your own choice. Do what makes you feel most comfortable. But in all cases, these issues have to be recognized, dealt with, and if we can keep our love for our kids foremost in our minds... hopefully peace will reign in providence.

I'll tell you one thing though, I'm looking at that Mencken quote with less cynicism and more alarm now, realizing how many people would really like to go along with the idea of eating missionaries.

Challenging the kids about their own behavior can be ticklish, especially when I deal with the subject of politics. I know, the unwritten rule, don't talk religion or politics. I know from friends, political differences have resulted in kids not talking to their parents, or not coming down to Florida for a Christmas vacation; however, I cannot let it go now, the stakes are too high. I just make sure whatever I say; I say it in a loving way.

Anonymous, father of six

I usually don't get in the middle of things, but I'm sorry, I just lost it over the border stuff, you know with the children.

Anonymous, mother of three

Something told me I shouldn't go. I just had a feeling my daughter's boyfriend's family and I, we weren't going to jell. So, I get there, and his eighty-year-old mother is watching a Trump rally on Fox News. Everyone at the rally is yelling: Lock her up! Lock her up! The mother is on her feet, yelling the same thing. I could have died. I bit my lip, stuck it out, and didn't say a word. You know what was the worst part? My daughter never came to my defense. She said I shouldn't get upset because she's an ignorant woman. I haven't seen in weeks.

Anonymous, mother of two

My daughter and her husband are on his side because his politics are more like his than mine, so there is no chance they can convince him to kiss and makeup with me.

Anonymous, mother of four

As far as Trump, she was holding herself together, wanted to say something to me, her liberal dad, but she didn't. Who knows what would have happened then?

Anonymous, father of one

They are completely opposite in their opinions, and I'm happy we did our job and raised independent thinkers.

T, mother of two

Sad stage of life now, with my daughter and me, and it's all because of the boyfriend. Not only does he admit he voted for Trump, but doesn't regret it. I'm crying my eyes out for those kids at the border, so how can I face him?

Anonymous, mother of two

Since her coming out, her politics have been extreme. She's over the top crazy. Alienated me, my boyfriend.

Anonymous, mother of one

Major problem if you let politics come between you and your kids. I'm keeping my views to myself, especially around my son-in-law and his mother. Harder for my husband, but if he just has a couple of drinks, he'll zone out.

Anonymous, mother of one

It's not one's finest moment. My aunt has disowned several Trump-voting cousins. My grandmother's niece has deleted every relation she suspects voted Republican. An uncle has apparently been mocking Clinton voters. Another uncle messaged me to gloat about taking the country back from 'libtards'. My grandparents have told me to ignore, and cut ties with racist family members. If America is divided, my family is in open civil war.

Anonymous, mother of two

My husband and I don't agree, so we try not to talk about it with our kids. We change the subject. We just stay away from it.

Anonymous, mother of two

I have friends who think differently from their kids, and it has resulted in the kids not talking to their parents. Like all things, when it comes to our kids, you have to pick your spots, talk to them carefully and with love.

Anonymous, father of six

They don't belong to you. They are persons.

S, mother of two

We don't talk politics. Relationships are more important.

Anonymous, mother of one

> *Don't ask a question you don't know the answer to.*
>
> —Jack McCoy, *Law and Order.*

Twenty-Four

Fact or Fiction
(The Rashomon Effect.)

*You have to acknowledge their memories,
eat crow if you have to.
Just make amends and go forward.*

—Anonymous, mother of two

I never considered writing a chapter on how memory adversely affects the relationship between parent and adult child, until a friend learned I was writing this book. He pulled me over, confided the biggest problem he had with his kids was that they remembered things he didn't believe were true, causing them to have bad feelings that negatively impacted their present-day relationships.

As he spoke, I thought of how my own daughter offhandedly mentioned that I was never home when she was growing up and I stammering back, "Who do you think took all the pictures of you in the playground?"

While I can point to the family photo album to prove my point, what I cannot deny is whatever else resides in her memory bank that may create an alternate reality from mine—one I must recognize forms the way she behaves toward me.

I keep thinking of the first sentence in *Anna Karenina:* "Happy families are all alike; every unhappy family is unhappy in its own way." I suspect Tolstoy was onto the same chink in our psychic armor Kurosawa so graphically captured a century later in *Rashomon.* We all live in our own realities and boy can that mess with our relationships.

On the bright side, one of my parents happily confessed, "I only saw it through their eyes much later." Let's all hope our eyesight gets that good.

*She remembers things that never happened.
I know that, because I was there.*

Anonymous, mother of two

*He told me he was sad growing up. Unbelievable.
His nickname was 'smiley'. Everybody thought
he was the happiest kid in the neighborhood.*

Anonymous, mother of two

*As a matter of fact, I had this discussion today! All
about our history and I said, that's your perspective,
and she said yes—and I'm right. (Laughter).*

H, mother of two

She has unresolved issues about her father, harbors a lot of anger toward me. My psychiatrist is helping me to understand this situation and showing me ways to deal with it. I still can't get over the fact that I worked like a dog to make sure they never did without, had food, clothing, travel and the best education. My son gets it, my daughter doesn't.

Anonymous, mother of two

When he was a little boy, a tradesperson or a neighbor mentioned how smart their child was. I said to my son, why aren't you a genius? He said, if you wanted me to be a genius, you should have been a genius yourself. It was a cruel and insensitive thing to say. To this day, I beat myself up because of it and I wonder if he remembers it?

P, mother of two

Don't talk ugly to them. Pull them aside, say there will be consequences, and you have to step up to the plate, make sure you live up to those threats. That is what my girls remember most and what they carry forward with their kids. I was just doing what my Momma did with me.

Anonymous, mother of two

Don't have that problem with my daughter, but with my son it has come up several times. Each time I apologize because, I obviously failed to communicate my true intentions. Otherwise, his perceptions wouldn't be totally different from my daughters' or mine.

Anonymous, father of two

My daughter had a particularly bad week. Somebody sideswiped her car. She made a party for her daughter, and her friends' mothers forgot to schedule it, so half the kids didn't show. She knows it's petty stuff, but still unsettling. My daughter says, she's trying to make her child responsible, but maybe she should have them lie and cheat to get through this life. I told her, I had the same thoughts about that when I was raising her and her brothers. Even now I sometimes beat myself over it. Did I do a disservice by trying to make them responsible, thoughtful of others and all those things nobody else was like that? You know what, after she vents, daughter smiles, tells me she's glad that's the way she is.

J, mother of six

Their memories are so different, and they have to be, because we didn't know half the stuff they did. Only recently, they told us when they got drunk they used to throw up out the window. We slept downstairs. They were on the second floor, so what did we know?

Anonymous, mother of eight

I know it's why I'm having trouble with my eldest daughter. When I tell her she's wrong, explain what really happened between her mother and me back when she was a teenager; she just shakes her head. It's all boiling over now because her mother and I have separated.

B, father of two

I never thought about it, either, until you just asked. I can see where it can be a problem. I think especially with my two kids. When they talk to me about their childhood, I get two different stories. In fact, my daughter is always complaining I enabled her brother, and that's what ruined him. I think she's jealous. It comes from when we sent him to a special school, because he was learning disabled. I offered to send her to a private school, for different reasons, she was really smart, but she said she liked it where she was. She won't admit it, but that's where I think the troubled started.

Anonymous, mother of two

Be honest with yourself. You may not like it, you may not believe it, but you have to recognize their recollections.

Anonymous, mother of two

Their perception at ten, and then at fifty, cannot be the same. But, it doesn't matter, because if their personalities don't allow them to be wrong, they will go to the wall with it.

Anonymous, father of two

I was the disciplinarian—my second husband was a marshmallow. I had my three, and he had one, his other two were adults and out of the house. One day, they said they wanted to have a business meeting with me. The next afternoon, we all sat down and they said, if you get a divorce, we want custody of him. Don't you know they still remind me of that day?

J, mother of six

Each of them saw it differently from each other, and from me. To hear them talk, it's like they grew up as if we were living in different worlds. Truly amazing.

M, mother of four

Her father's death left so many marks. She wasn't able to deal with it then, or now, but to this day, she will not explain herself to me. I just have to wait.

Anonymous, mother of two

Growing up I thought she was my best friend. She was the easiest kid. The one I could talk to most openly. Turns out at the age of fifty she tells me she had a horrible childhood, that she was faking it up to then; felt neglected, not loved. Stuff that kept coming out was totally insane. Hadn't the slightest inkling. She didn't speak to me for three years after that. Even now, we have a tenuous relationship. Still can't believe she faked it all those years.

Anonymous, mother of four

I heard from other parents they have had experiences so different than their children. I suspect, if you got all families together, it would be really interesting to hear them describe their childhood, what it was like growing up and I bet you would get similar results. What a revelation that would be!

M, mother of four

Over the years she comes up with things that never happened. I don't know how to deal with it. My husband, says, just let it go. Right now, I have no other choice.

Anonymous, mother of two

She had ten kids, even wanted to adopt more. From the outside we all saw the perfect all-American, mid-western family. Father made good money. Big beautiful house in the suburbs. Kids all got a good education. When

We Gave Them Life, Now They're Trying To Take Ours

you hear the kids speak about their childhood, absolute horror. Totally dysfunctional family according to them. Learned later, the mother was an alcoholic. Another big surprise! Can you imagine with their recollections, how they could have related to their alcoholic mom?

M, mother of four

I have three kids and a husband. They were all in the house. They all saw it differently. My youngest two saw the bickering directed at my eldest. My eldest thought I was yelling at my husband, and at her. I didn't think there was any yelling. Perhaps, because I come from a family that yelled—but out of love. That was how they, we, communicated. My husband doesn't remember anything. Oh, and my two youngest, they don't agree about me cooking dinner every night. My boy says I did, which I did—and my girl doesn't remember it.

Anonymous, mother of three

Bottom line, this is how our conversation about her growing up goes. I used to yell a lot. I don't think I did. Yes, you did!

Anonymous, mother of three

She made up a story that I hit her with a wooden spoon, even broke it once when I hit her. I used to hit my son on the backside with one, never hard enough to break it. Once, after he knew he'd done something wrong, he handed it to me. I put it away, vowed never to do it again.

Anonymous, mother of two

Oh, I remember why you beat me up. Forty years ago when my daughter was a kid and did something nasty, I hit her in the ass. Not hard, not even a whack. When we talk it about it, what she really says is that I insulted her dignity.

Anonymous, father of two

When they blame me for what happened in the past, I don't get upset anymore. I feel our relationship is still a work in progress.

H, mother of three

Need to listen. You might not like what they say, but you must think about it, dissect it, and be honest with yourself in order to accept it as their reality. You may have to humble yourself if you are going to have a productive second dialogue that will result in some forward movement.

Anonymous, mother of two

We have many discussions about this very topic, and I've thought about what she said, how she remembers events. I told her that I'm sorry, that she was right, that I should have been more accessible to her. I'm glad we could talk about it now, as adults, who know there was, and is, love between us.

K, mother of one

He was always complimentary to me, my cooking. When he moved out, he confronted me as an adult, complained that there was always so much screaming going on. Made him uncomfortable. I said, "Wow!" Never realized that. Had a follow-up meeting with his two sisters who said it was true — there was a lot of screaming. I had them too close together, lots of confusion going on. Probably from their perspective, my trying to get things done, there was a lot of yelling, a lot of drama. Tell your kids what I told mine. I did it out of love. I did the best I could.

Anonymous, mother of one

How important is your relationship? If it is important, and if you don't accept their criticism, you can acknowledge it by simply saying that was the last thing in my life I wanted you to believe.

S, mother of two

My daughter and son can tell the story of their childhood in two completely different ways. Actually, we have three opinions of what actually happened—

theirs and ours—my husband and mine. We make a joke out of it. What else can you do, it's humorous.

Anonymous, mother of two

They won't admit they're wrong about what they remember because it's such a strong part of who they are now.

Anonymous, father of two

Out of the blue, she tells me she hated me when she was growing up because I was always the center of attraction. I told her I wasn't. To prove it, I had her aunts and her cousins speak to her. Didn't change her mind. She said I stole the light away from her. Thank God that's behind us and we are okay now.

Anonymous, mother of two

We pretty much agree on everything except when her father was ill and dying. She was of the opinion he became distant because he couldn't cope with growing old, perhaps not feeling totally healthy, and unable to do the things he used to do. I don't think she wanted to see or remember that he was seriously ill and dying.

Anonymous, mother of one

If you ask my son, he'd tell you what he remembers most of his childhood is every Friday night, I took him for pizza. That's exactly what I did because I tried to give each one of my children a piece of me alone. As far as the rest of their memories, all pretty much the same as mine, no major discrepancies have come up to interfere with our present relationships.

Anonymous, mother of three

I would say we have the same memories but different feelings about the events.

Anonymous, mother of six

Even though we haven't shared those memories, I always thought that when they get older, they might have some insight into their behavior. We could get together and talk about it, see if we all remembered the same things, or maybe when I'm in the hospital, lying in my bed with tubes sticking into me. (Laughter)

Anonymous, father of two

They perceive me as bossy, but I haven't been that way in twenty years. They also think I would disapprove of their lives now, or what they do, but I don't.

Anonymous, mother of three

She brought them up to think, where the hell is he? No wonder my kids don't remember me being there for them.

Anonymous, father of two

Kids react to us now based on the past and things that happened then to make them nervous. If they see them again, now, or something similar, there is tension—that it could be a signal to them those things are not as good as I think they are.

Anonymous, mother of two

People see, hear things differently, and you have to expect that. You have to accept and work through it.

Anonymous, mother of one

I'm always looking for reasons why my son became alienated and perhaps it had to do with him not really being accepted into his stepfather's family the way he thought he would be. My second husband had two boys, and I think my son was very disappointed that they didn't become his best friends. I may be grasping at straws because we never talked about it.

Anonymous, mother of two

My youngest has memories of my tiny studio and she realized she does have a connection with me— that I gave her art; but there was no thank you, just a matter-of-fact statement.

Anonymous, father of two

> *Memories are what warm you up from the inside. But they're also what tear you apart.*
>
> —Haruki Murakam

Twenty-Five

Cats Among The Pigeons
(Mothers and Daughters)

When did it start?
How about as soon as she took her first breath?

—Anonymous, mother of two

Okay, I confess—it's probably because I'm not a mother that I didn't immediately realize this familial relationship merited its own chapter.

Happily, it only took two interviews to understand that whether we were discussing the topic of health, or finance, the incendiary nature of that maternal link took center stage, and was the cause of the catastrophic discord that ensued.

I know all mothers can't relate to this toxicity. You have been blessed. Don't pat yourself on the back too quickly because the next chapter deals with fathers who think their daughters walk on water and this may be your Achilles heel.

Again, my interviews exposed the good, the bad, and the ugly of this topic. It's up to you to identify with one, if not all, of those experiences. As always, try to look for the positive. Take what you can to improve your relationships. If you think tattooing your daughter's name over your heart will prove you love her, do it! Just make sure it's permanent, because reconciliation can come undone as quickly as a fake tattoo washes away in a swimming pool.

So much craziness with my daughter, it sent me back to therapy.

Anonymous, mother of two

In my opinion, much more difficult, much more stress dealing with daughters than sons. I don't want to call it a competition, although many of my friends do.

Anonymous, mother of two

She told me she loved me, but didn't want to have anything more to do with me, or the family. My only comfort, if you call it that, is that every mother I speak with is having serious problems with their daughters.

Anonymous, mother of two

When both my kids were young, I told them I'm your mother, not your friend. When my daughter was in her forties, I sat her down and we had a conversation. I said we are on the same level and we can be friends. I guess, because it has been a more difficult relationship, I chose her to talk with, not my son with whom I've had a much easier time of it.

Anonymous, mother of two

I don't have any sons, so I don't know if it's a mother and daughter thing. I just know with her, I don't add anything to the conversation. Why? Because she always took whatever I said in a negative way so now I just smile, and say, that's great.

Anonymous, mother of one

Can anyone really know? Jealousy, envy, never had any of those emotions. For instance, her beauty, intelligence, or professional career—they far surpassed mine and I can honestly say I am thrilled. Our issues? She keeps everything to herself. Then again, I never confided to my mother.

Anonymous, mother of one

My mother always made me feel good. Even after I got married. Our relationship never changed. We could talk to each other about anything. That's what I expected with my daughter and until my second husband arrived, that's the kind of relationship we had. Everything changed when I married X. Now, whatever I say is received in a negative way and she takes it as a criticism. I guess it's jealously? What's really odd is she and X get along very well. She talks to him about everything, listens to every bit of advice he gives her. I know I have to stop feeling sorry for myself. Stop wishing for, or wondering why, I don't have the relationship with my daughter that I had with my own mother.

Anonymous, mother of one

I always thought it was her jealousy of her brother that caused the rift because it still comes up when she talks to me, which is now infrequent at best. Thinking about your question, perhaps it is more of a mother/daughter thing, because she never had a problem with her father or stepfather.

Anonymous, mother of two

My relationship with my two girls is more real than the one with my mother. We talk about everything. With my mom, there was a divide between mother and child. I think it had to do with the times and how parents were parenting. It had nothing to do with the love they gave me, or I felt.

Anonymous, mother of two

> By the time a woman realizes
> her mother was right,
> she has a daughter who thinks she's wrong.
>
> —Anonymous

Twenty-Six

She Walks On Water
(Daddy's Little Girl)

*She could do no wrong.
How's that for how I saw their relationship?*

—Anonymous, mother of one

(WARNING! FULL DISCLOSER—MY DAUGHTER DOES NOT WALK ON WATER—SHE GLIDES!)

Okay—now that I got that off my chest, let's get on with this important topic in a fair, balanced and objective way.

I know you mothers out there are shaking your collective heads. How can I, or any of the fathers I interviewed, be objective? You think we're all just silly putty in the hands of our manipulative, mischievous, and all too often, malevolent daughters masquerading as sugarplums.

Well, let's just see if I can prove you doubting Thomasina wrong, and show you there is nothing over my orbs when it comes to presenting that fair, balanced and objective chapter I talked about.

To that end, I'm asking my fellow Dads to go easy on Photoshop. Halos are okay, but no more angel wings.

From the time she was born, I was the bad guy. He just washed his hands and let me get all the grief. Is that why he can do no wrong and I'm always to blame? Is that the reason, or is it female rivalry? My shrink won't give me an answer, just tells me to deal with it.

Anonymous, mother of one

He just does whatever they want. He's the good guy. I'm the bad guy.

Anonymous, mother of two

I only have girls, but I think I treated them as I would a boy except I would have played a little rougher and supported his desire to play high school and college football like I did.

Anonymous, father of two

I don't think it's a daddy thing. I just understand her better than anyone else because I have similar traits in my personality.

Anonymous, father of six

She talks to me about finances, talks to her mom about other things. Soft spot for her, sure she's my baby girl, but I don't see any difference between how me, or my wife, deal with her.

J, father of two

My daughter and I are close, but she has an amazing relationship with her mom. Is it a mother/daughter thing? Probably.

Anonymous, father of two

Oh, definitely. Even with my second husband. And you know what, she must sense that she's special because whatever he says, and it may be the same suggestion, advice I've given her, never does she get mad at him, thinks it's critical.

Anonymous, mother of one

He would always say to me, you discipline her. I won't because she gets upset and I don't want to see her upset. So, I was the bad guy.

Anonymous, mother of two

I can't be certain, but I think I treated my daughters the same, had, I had boys. Maybe softer because I didn't play rough sports with them.

Anonymous, father of two

I have had no communications to speak of with my two girls for over thirty years and it is because my ex wife poisoned them against me. I also have to say they take after her, and her scheming ways, so when there is communication, I don't get overly emotional because I don't want to expose myself to potential disappointment, that has happened in the past.

Anonymous, father of two

Remove yourself from the situation. My wife calls it apathy.

Anonymous, father of one

Sometimes it's hard to deal with a person, know how to deal with them. It's even harder for me because they are of the opposite sex. On top of that, they are my blood. Maybe that's why I left it to my wife to be the disciplinarian?

S, father of two

The key is how you deliver your intentions, your message. It goes for my wife and for my daughter… for anyone, really.

N, father of two

> *I think my mom put it best. She said, 'Little girls soften their daddy's hearts.'*
>
> —Paul Walker

Twenty-Seven

Death Comes To Us All
(Hush, Hush.)

I thought I was the only one afraid to mention this subject to my kids. Boy, was I wrong.

—*The Author*

If I haven't already stated it, or if you haven't already guessed, I'm writing this book as much for myself, as for other parents; asking the same questions, seeking the same answers, looking for the same validation and hoping to learn how they can become a better parent to their adult children.

Case in point, this chapter. It was of great comfort to discover I wasn't alone in my fears, but even more critical to learn, despite one's trepidations; we can have this conversation if we understand how to address everyone's fears in a calm and mature fashion.

I know—if pigs could fly they'd be eagles and I wouldn't have had to write this book. Nevertheless, it's important to be constantly reminded of how vital it is to consider their emotions, so that you can allay their fears and set the stage for a reassuring, nonthreatening and constructive conversation.

FYI—if you're planning to tell them you intend to be cryogenically frozen, first get a sense of whether they're looking forward to your next birthday, because if they're not....

The easiest way to get the kids to visit you right before a holiday is to call them and bring up the subject of dying. Either they are terrified you'll die and make them orphans, or they are equally afraid you will leave them out of your will, (She laughs)

Anonymous, mother of four

Just don't put me in the ground. I made them swear. I'm even thinking about putting it into my will.

Anonymous, mother of three

People will abandon you by death. You better get used to that. You better make a life for yourself. I tried to teach them that.

Anonymous, mother of four

Every time I bring it up, they shut me down. I don't blame them. Talking about my death isn't very comfortable.

Anonymous, father of one

We talk to them about our wills because it's realistic. Sure, it bothers them to talk about death, even indirectly.

Anonymous, mother of two

Our relationship is so bad that I want to end it with him. I feel so sad and left out, that's the way he makes me feel. Maybe I should tell him how I feel before I pass on. I think I'd be better off. I know I'm not answering your question, but this is how I feel.

Anonymous, mother of two

I had my mother, their grandmother tell them—I just couldn't. We all went over to her house. She's ninety-one, but still has all her faculties, takes care of herself. We all cried, then we laughed. We all had milk and homemade cookies.

Anonymous, mother of three

Eric Robespierre

I enable them terribly. It's so bad my husband is always threatening to leave me. If I brought up this subject, he says they would only ask for money. That would be the last straw, don't you think?

Anonymous, mother of three

I brought the subject up when they came over for the holidays and we were watching one of those zombie movies. You're not going to put this in, are you? (She laughs) Oh, it doesn't matter. Anyway, it worked out. It was a real icebreaker. (She laughs)

Anonymous, mother of two

Now, this is funny. We were in her kitchen when my grandson asked me if I was ever going to die. I nearly had a heart attack. Bless his heart, he hugged me, said he'd miss me. Later, my daughter got me alone, and we had a serious discussion. I can't believe I had been so afraid to bring it up.

Anonymous, mother of one

One of my boys brought the subject up. My daughter had to leave the room. It was a mess but after we all had a couple of stiff drinks, we talked it out.

I have no advice for other parents, except maybe have a couple before the subject comes up.

Anonymous, mother of two

The most important thing that parents can teach their children is how to get along without them.

—Frank Clark

Twenty-Eight

The Takeaway
(Before They Take Us Away, Away.)

*I feel better after I talked to you.
Maybe there is a way forward.*

—Anonymous, father of two

If you've gotten this far, you must have identified with one or more of the parents and the stories they had to tell. Wondered if it's a gene you were born with, or you bought it at an auction, but you always want to fix everything, even if your kids are in their fifties.

Maybe you're in your seventies and have finally realized you're just playing the cards you were dealt with; and thankful, your children are still alive and still talking to you.

Maybe you're metaphorically running round and round the mulberry bush trying to make sense of your relationships, and the only thing you got for your troubles are headaches, heartburn and heartaches.

We Gave Them Life, Now They're Trying To Take Ours

I hope, after reading this book you're like the parent quoted up top—feeling better and maybe seeing a way forward.

The one important thing I've learned… you can solve a lot of problems if you just get your kids over to the house and watch a good zombie movie.

Don't ask too many questions; you may not like the answers.

J, father of two

To go hand in hand, together. To practice forgiveness. To forgive yourself. I can deal with anything then.

SH, mother of two

I see my downfalls and I am aware of them.

B, mother of one

I will always be protective of him because he was a twin and the other one died.

P, mother of two

You love them. You admire them, and it's part of life.

C, mother of three

You play the hand you were dealt, plain and simple.

Anonymous, mother of three

They are a mixed bag. I really enjoy them in my retirement. Adds a little spice to my life.

Anonymous, father of six

I'm of the sandwich generation. When I was growing up I had to listen to what my parents said. We cared about what they said. You wanted to please them. In my kid's generation, we had to be careful what we said to them, so they would like us, be around us. We didn't want to hurt them, be the reason they had to lie on a psychiatrist's couch. They didn't care what we said. See what I mean, being in a sandwich between those two generations? Now, this present generation, they are even more indulged.

J, mother of six

Parents should let their children go; they really should. Just detach. Can you believe I was packing my twenty-eight-year-olds travel bag?

B, mother of one

Be mindful. Don't struggle with what ifs. Accept and be open. My daughter is now like my mother, telling me in the sweetest way, don't do that, or do this.

N, mother of two

I just recently cut the umbilical cord. Just did it. Until then, I was just putting myself in her life and had to step away. May have been too late. She just turned forty this fall.

B, mother of one

I don't know what I did to make her think I did not want to have a relationship. That thought keeps me up at night.

Anonymous, father of two

If you give a shit, you have to break down that wall that separates you from them. There is no easy answer on how to do that, but first you must recognize the problem. Otherwise, if you let it block you, there will be no relationship.

Anonymous, father of one

Accept, acknowledge, perhaps change; even humble yourself if that is your last resort.

S, mother of two

*Whatever he says to her, she laughs it off.
Whatever I say, she criticizes. Go figure.*

P, mother of two

*I'm a black and white person. I can't see the grey.
I know this is a problem and I'm working on it.*

Anonymous, mother of two

They were brought up to respect us and we set a good example. You set a good example and you won't have any problems. Dinner was always on the table at a certain time. I did all the laundry. They were expected to help. All had summer jobs and the money they earned contributed to their needs. That's the way I was brought up.

Anonymous, mother of eight

My eldest came down and we went to the beach. When she went into the water I watched her like a hawk. Just like I did when she was learning and now she swims better than I ever could. When she came out she said I saw you watching me. I said you're always a mother and a child is forever.

Anonymous, mother of three

My daughter, from the time she was in nursery school, always kept secrets from me. She separated her world from mine. Created a wall, boundaries. I can respect that. I need my space, too. However, she has shut me out during times I could have helped her with her problems.

Anonymous, mother of one

You always worry about your kids. It's a lifelong thing.

C, mother of three

We communicate very well. I don't tell her what to do and all is good.

S, mother of one

The family unit, as we know it, will not be what it is in years to come.

P, mother of two

My son finally confessed the part he played, and I said he had to forgive himself. Then I said, I needed some space, time to process the situation. He said I was closing the door on him. I said I didn't want to say something I couldn't take back.

Anonymous, mother of three

Eric Robespierre

Try to let them lead their own lives. Try not to get overly involved. Try to let them make their own decisions, without you, making any judgments. Just let them live. Not easy. Sometimes you want to give them your opinion. Unless they are physically or mentally impaired, let them live their own lives.

N, mother of two

The way I look at it, it's like baking a chocolate cake and you cut off three equal slices. The first child says I love chocolate cake, but I'm allergic to it and I'm going to break out in hives. The second one says I hate it. The third says, oh Mommy, I love chocolate cake, and it makes my tummy feel oh, so good. You have to deal with each kid differently, because what I'm saying is — there is no formula, even when they grow to be adults.

J, mother of six

It was their life. I tried to steer them in a certain direction, to certain values, but you can't make people a certain way. They develop in that way and it is what it is.

M, mother of four

Once your children become adults, we as parents have to be put into a cupboard and kept there;

*staying nice and quiet, until the time comes
when they need us and then we come out.*

> Anonymous, mother of two

Who knows what's at the end of the diving board?

> J, mother of two

You can't feel guilty about how you raised your kids. Be more concerned with how you deal with your own life now.

> Anonymous, mother of four

I really don't have problems with my children. They like me, they really do. I don't take any credit. This is the way they are. DNA wins. I really think that.

> S, mother of two

When he was a little boy he had mood swings, but he would always come up to our room and apologize. Ask if I always would love him. I said yes. Even if I killed someone? I told him I would be terribly disappointed that he would do such a horrible thing but, because I was his mommy, I would always love him. Now, that we are estranged because of his wife, or whatever, I still hear myself saying those words to myself.

> Anonymous, mother of two

If, after I hear them out, and they are hurt by what they thought I say, I apologize. I don't get defensive. I don't argue with how they remember stuff. I do know that I should have been more accessible when they were younger. Perhaps that was the cause of it. I don't see our talks now as who is right or wrong, or who's at fault; instead as an adult way to communicate feelings in a healthy and healing way. Let me add, I don't blame myself for my actions. I thought I was right at the time. Of course, I don't tell them that. I'm telling you so you tell other parents they shouldn't blame themselves. They did what they did at the time.

H, mother of three

If it's beneficial to your life, just do it. Will that be at the expense of others—your child for instance? That's your dilemma, that's your decision.

Anonymous, mother of one

Being a teacher has helped me understand and respect a child's differences. This experience helped me with my relationship with my own children, especially when they were younger.

Anonymous, mother of two

He suddenly got too busy for me when he got married. No question it was she but I'm disappointed he didn't stand up for himself. Who knew?

Anonymous, mother of two

I had to be mother, father, sister, brother, best friend... it was a terrible responsibility. You always have to be on your toes. Being the perfect person to give them the best information, get them involved, enhance their lives and their growth, and I had to do it myself. If you do all that, I can tell you it does not guarantee a healthy, loving relationship now, when they are adults.

S, mother of two

It's easy to blame others, when it's you having the problem.

Anonymous, mother of two

Don't ask any questions, and don't make any comments. That's my advice to any parent of grownup children. When did I learn this? A year and a half ago at my daughter's fortieth! Took me seventeen years! Not very bright, huh? (She laughs)

Anonymous, mother of one

Eric Robespierre

At first you have to see them as they are and separate from yourself. Then you have to come to terms with who they are. Then do two things. Accept them as individuals and second, much harder, support them for who are and what they want to do.

E, mother of one

No questions, no accusations.

Anonymous, mother of one

You cannot set rules that stop them from becoming individuals with their own way of doing things. It follows that when they are adults and achieved that independence, you respect it and their privacy.

Anonymous, mother of three

You have to stand back and watch them live their lives. If you see them going over the cliff, that's a different story.

S, mother of two

They are always looking for signals; we are not as good as we think we are.

Anonymous, mother of two

*I always thought, as a clinical psychologist, when
I became a mother, I would know what I needed to do to
stimulate their growth. No matter what was happening,
because of my training, I'd be such a good mother
I would make them feel stable and safe. I was wrong.*

Anonymous, mother of two

*I'm not their therapist and they're not mine.
Definite boundaries need to be maintained
in order to have a normal relationship.*

Anonymous, mother of two

*Not sure what you can do after they become adults.
I think you build loving relationships at birth. I did
it by never treating them as infants, used whole
words and always thought of them as individuals.
Always talked about why you want to do it your way,
see if we could come to a mutual conclusion.*

Anonymous, mother of three

*I gave my kids what I never had growing in an
orphanage... a family! And, I made damn sure
we would never ever be separated like I was.*

Anonymous, mother of three

You cannot be a good parent if you cannot provide a loving home. This is the foundation that you and they build.

Anonymous, mother of two

Your children develop free will and you cannot be responsible for their behavior. You may have done things that were wrong, but their teachers, peer group, also influenced them. So many influences on a kid's life you cannot take responsibility for how they turn out. What mother has told her kids to drink and take drugs? Nobody has.

Anonymous, mother of two

If you have hurt them, it is unusual if your kids understand where you have been coming from. All you can say to yourself is… I did the best I could but I may have hurt them indirectly. It was the best I could do in that moment I was, in but I know I could do a lot better if I had a do-over.

Anonymous, mother of two

We created these people. If they're short with us, ignoring us, mean to us, we have to figure out what we did and what we can do better.

Anonymous, mother of two

I don't like his wife. There is always a backstory to the backstory to the backstory.

        Anonymous, mother of two

When I worked on myself, watched how I talked, learned to listen more, my relationship with my son improved and became even more warm and loving.

        Anonymous, mother of one

I thought I could make up for the difficulties I had with my husband by being such a good mother. Doesn't work.

        Anonymous, mother of two

I remember hearing, 'A father holds his daughter's hand for a short while, but he holds her heart forever'. That about sums it up for me.

        Anonymous, father of one

Character, personality comes from DNA and nurturing. We have some control over the nurture part; if you have guilt about protecting them more, know you did the best you could.

        Anonymous, mother of two

I know some parents will say how can you love one child more than another, but I love her more because she is a part of my life and he isn't.

Anonymous, mother of two

I raised him on my own. His father was never around. I couldn't have done it without an extended family—my father, my brothers.

Anonymous, mother of one

I think I mentioned this to you on another subject but I have to say it again. Most advice falls on deaf ears. I don't mean to be negative, just practical and rational.

Anonymous, mother of two

Sometimes it's hard to deal with a person, your child. Their personality can blow you over. You have to remove yourself from the situation to make it work. Then, if you do want to communicate your thoughts, feelings, it has to be the right delivery. That's the key. How do you deliver your intentions, your message without them, as I said, blowing you over? And, it has to come naturally. Pretty hard stuff, huh?

Anonymous, mother of two

I hadn't spoken to my younger daughter who is forty-three, in over fifteen years, until she emailed me to wish me a happy birthday. She also hoped I have a nice life and that everything was fine. I wrote her back, but have not heard from her again, so I am not sure if we will have anything like a constant communication.

Anonymous, father of two

They're in their fifties and they still keep me up at night, worrying. But it's a good kind of worrying. I really don't know what I'm saying, Crazy, huh?

Anonymous, mother of three

If somebody hasn't already said it, I'll say it —it's a crapshoot. You don't know what you're getting when they're born. Have no idea how they are going to react to you and your husband. They get out into the world— no clue as to how that will turn out.

Anonymous, mother of three

> *It doesn't take a lot to let go of your child. It takes everything.*
>
> —Fredrik Backman, *A Man Called Ove*

> *If you've never been hated by your child, you've never been a parent.*
>
> —Bette Davis

> *They fuck you up, your mum and dad.*
> *They may not mean to, but they do.*
> *They fill you with the faults they*
> *had and add some extra,*
> *just for you.*
> *But they were fucked up in their turn*
> *by fools in old-style hats and coats,*
> *who half the time were soppy-stern*
> *and half at one another's throats.*
>
> —*Philip Larkin*

About the Author

Eric Robespierre was born and raised in New York City. He has worked as a screenwriter, playwright, documentary film director and web designer. He has been an award winning advertising copywriter creating campaigns for Mitsubishi, Izod Lacoste, and other major brands.

Robespierre is now a full-time writer. Together with Helen Brand he wrote *The Yummy Hunter's Guide: The Best-Tasting, Low-Calorie Foods and Where to Shop for Them.* He is also the author of *Cracking the Walnut: How Being a Little Nuts Helped Me to Beat Prostate Cancer*, *Living Large in America: The Life and Times of the Family Ginsburg (Pronounced Du Pont)*: *Lighten Up And Log In For Love: How Humor Helps Baby Boomers Survive Online Dating*, and *We Gave Them Life, Now They're Trying To Take Ours: How To Talk To Adult Children Before It's Too Late.*

Visit Eric Robespierre at:
www.ericrobespierre.com

www.ingramcontent.com/pod-product-compliance
Lightning Source LLC
LaVergne TN
LVHW051227080426
835513LV00016B/1452